LEAVINGTHEFOLD

LEAVINGTHEFOLD

Apostates and Defectors in Antiquity

STEPHEN G. WILSON

FORTRESS PRESS
MINNEAPOLIS

LEAVING THE FOLD
Apostates and Defectors in Antiquity

Jacket design: Kevin van der Leek Design Inc.
Jacket art: Two men in a boat. Relief, 3rd Century. Rome © Erich Lessing/Art Resource, NY
Book Design: James Korsmo

Library of Congress Cataloging-in-Publication Data

Wilson, S. G. (Stephen G.)
 Leaving the fold : apostates and defectors in antiquity / Stephen G. Wilson.
  p. cm.
 Includes bibliographical references (p.   ) and indexes.
 ISBN 0-8006-3675-9 (alk. paper)
 1. Apostasy—Christianity—History. 2. Church history—Primitive and early church, ca. 30-600. 3. Apostasy—Judaism—History. I. Title.
 BT1319.W55 2004
 204'.2—dc22

2004015485

The paper used in this publication meets the minimum requirements of American National Standard for Information Sciences — Permanence of Paper for Printed Library Materials, ANSI Z329.48-1984.

Manufactured in the U.S.A.

08   07   06   05   04   1   2   3   4   5   6   7   8   9   10

To Ellen, Liam, and others to come

CONTENTS

PREFACE

In recent years, I have occasionally heard it said that a discussion of apostasy remains a desideratum. This is less true of Judaism, where one or two notable studies have appeared, but in studies of early Christianity and the world of pagan polytheism, it undoubtedly remains the case. My modest aim is to draw attention to as broad a range of evidence as I could find for apostasy and to discuss some of its implications. It is only a start, and I hope it will provoke others to think about the topic too. I have learned a great deal from Professor J. G. Barclay's work on the Jewish evidence, and wish to acknowledge the use of his diagrams in the conclusion.

Briefer versions of this study were commented on by Alan Segal, Nicola Denzy, and Margaret MacDonald at a meeting of the Canadian Society of Biblical Studies, and Martin Goodman was kind enough to look over parts of it too. I am grateful for their comments.

My wife, Jennifer, as usual contributed to matters of style, consistency, and sense with her skillful copyediting.

The book is dedicated to our grandchildren, who light up our lives.

ABBREVIATIONS

Ancient Sources

1QH	*Hodayot* (Hymn Scroll)
1QM	*Milḥamah* (War Scroll)
1QpHab	Habakkuk Commentary
1QS	*Serek ha-Yaḥad* (Community Rule)
4QMMT	Halakic Letter
4QpNah	Nahum Commentary
4QTest	Testimonia (4Q 175)
11QT	Temple Scroll (11Q 19)
Avod. Zar.	*Avodah Zarah*
Acts Phil.	*Acts of Philip*
Apuleius, *Apol.*	*Apologia (Apology)*
Athenagoras, *Leg.*	*Legatio pro Christianis*
b.	Babylonian Talmud *(Bavli)*
Bek.	*Bekorot*
Ber.	*Berakot*
B. Metz.	*Baba Metzia*
Caesar	
Bell. civ.	*Bellum civile (Civil War)*
Bell. gall.	*Bellum gallicum (Gallic War)*
Cicero	
Acad.	*Academicae quaestiones*
Luc.	*Lucullus* (in *Academici Priora*)
Nat. d.	*De natura deorum*
Phil.	*Orationes philippicae*
Pis.	*In Pisonem*
Sest.	*Pro Sestio*
Sull.	*Pro Sulla*
Tusc.	*Tusculanae disputationes*
Diodorus Siculus, *Bib. hist.*	*Bibliotheca historica (Library of History)*
Diog. L.	Diogenes Laertius
Ep.	*Epistle*
Eruv.	*Eruvin*

Eusebius
    Dem. ev.   *Demonstratio evangelica (Demonstration of the Gospel)*

    Hist. eccl.   *Historia ecclesiastica (Ecclesiastical History)*

Giṭ.   *Giṭṭin*
Gregory of Nyssa, *Eun.*   *Contra Eunomium (Against Eunomius)*
Ḥag.   *Ḥagigah*
Herm.   *Shepherd of Hermas*
    Sim.   *Similitude*
    Vis.   *Vision*
Herodotus, *Hist.*   *Historiae (Histories)*
Hor.   *Horayot*
Ḥul.   *Ḥullin*
Iamblichus, *VP*   *Vita Pythagorica (On the Pythagorean Way of Life)*

Ignatius of Antioch
    Eph.   *Letter to the Ephesians*
    Trall.   *Letter to the Trallians*
Ind. Acad.   *Index Academicorum*
Irenaeus, *Haer.*   *Adversus haereses (Against Heresies)*
Josephus
    Ag. Ap.   *Against Apion*
    Ant.   *Jewish Antiquities*
    Life   *The Life*
    War   *Jewish War*
Jub.   *Jubilees*
Julian, *Ag. Gal.*   *Against the Galileans*
Justin Martyr
    Dial.   *Dialogus cum Tryphone (Dialogue with Trypho)*

    1 Apol.   *First Apology*
Lucian
    Hermot.   *Hermotimus*
    Peregr.   *Passing of Peregrinus*
LXX   Septuagint
m.   Mishnah

Mart. Pol.	Martyrdom of Polycarp
Meg.	Megillah
Mo'ed Qaṭ.	Mo'ed Qaṭan
Origen, Cels.	Contra Celsum (Against Celsus)
Philo Judaeus	
Abr.	De Abrahamo (On the Life of Abraham)
Agr.	De agricultura (On Agriculture)
Conf.	De confusione linguarum (On the Confusion of Tongues)
Conteml.	De vita contemplativa (On the Contemplative Life)
Ebr.	De ebrietate (On Drunkenness)
Flacc.	In Flaccum (Against Flaccus)
Fug.	De fuga et inventione (On Flight and Finding)
Ios.	De Iosepho (On the Life of Joseph)
Leg.	Legum allegoriae (Allegorical Interpretation)
Legat.	Legatio ad Gaium (On the Embassy to Gaius)
Plant.	De plantatione (On Planting)
Migr.	De migratione Abrahamo (On the Migration of Abraham)
Mos.	De vita Mosis (On the Life of Moses)
Mut.	De mutatione nominum (On the Change of Names)
Opif.	De opificio mundi (On the Creation of the World)
Post.	De posteritate Caini (On the Posterity of Cain)
Praem.	De praemiis et poenis (On Rewards and Punishments)
QG	Quaestiones et solutiones in Genesin (Questions and Answers on Genesis)
Sobr.	De sobrietate (On Sobriety)
Spec.	De specialibus legibus (On the Special Laws)
Virt.	De virtutibus (On the Virtues)

Pliny the Younger, *Ep.*	*Epistulae* (*Letters*)
Plutarch	
Rom.	*Romulus*
Mor.	*Moralia*
Rosh Hash.	*Rosh Hashanah*
Sanh.	*Sanhedrin*
Sextus Empiricus, *Pyr.*	*Pyrrhoniae hypotyposes* (*Outlines of Pyrrhonism*)
Shabb.	*Shabbat*
Sheqal.	*Sheqalim*
Socrates, *Hist. eccles.*	*Historia ecclesiastica*
Suetonius	
Dom.	*Domitianus*
Tib.	*Tiberius*
t.	Tosefta
Tacitus	
Ann.	*Annales* (*Annals*)
Hist.	*Historiae* (*Histories*)
Tatian, *Or. Graec.*	*Oratio Graecae* (*Greek Orations*)
Tertullian	
Mart.	*Ad martyras* (*To the Martyrs*)
Praescr.	*De praescriptione haereticorum* (*Prescription against Heretics*)
Res.	*De resurrectione carnis* (*The Resurrection of the Flesh*)
Ux.	*Ad uxorem* (*To His Wife*)
Val.	*Adversus Valentinianos* (*Against the Valentinians*)
TLG	*Thesaurus Lingua Graeca*
y.	Jerusalem Talmud (*Yerushalmi*)
Yev.	*Yevamot*

Modern Sources

AGJU	Arbeiten zur Geschichte des antiken Judentums und Urchristentums
ANRW	*Aufstieg und Niedergang der römischen Welt: Geschichte und Kultur Roms im Spiegel der neueren Forschung*, edited by H. Temporini and W. Haase, Berlin, 1972–
BibIntSer	Biblical Interpretation Series
BO	*Bibliotheca orientalis*
BJS	Brown Judaic Studies
CCCA	*Corpus cultus Cybellae Attidisque: 1. Asia minor*, translated by M. J. Vermaseren (Leiden: Brill, 1987)
CIG	*Corpus inscriptionum graecarum*, edited by August Boeckh et al., 4 vols., 1828–77
CII	*Corpus inscriptionum iudaicarum*, vol. I (1936), vol. II (1952), edited by J. B. Frey. Vol. I (= *CII* I²) revised with prolegomenon by B. Lifshitz (New York: Ktav, 1975)
CIL	*Corpus inscriptionum latinarum*, edited by T. Mommsen, E. Lommatzsch, A. Degrassi, and A.U. Stylow (Berlin: Reimer, 1893)
CPJ	*Corpus papyrorum judaicorum*, edited by V. Tcherikover, 3 vols. (Cambridge, 1957–64)
CRINT	Compendia rerum iudaicarum ad Novum Testamentum
CSHJ	Chicago Studies in the History of Judaism
EJ	*The Encyclopaedia of Judaism*, edited by Geoffrey Wigoder, 1989
EncJud	*Encyclopaedia Judaica*, 16 vols., Jerusalem, 1972

EncTal	*Encyclopaedia Talmudica*, 3 vols., 1969–78
HTR	*Harvard Theological Review*
HUCA	*Hebrew Union College Annual*
IGRR	*Inscriptiones graecae ad res romanes per-tinentes*, edited by René Cagnat et al., 4 vols., 1901–27
JBL	*Journal of Biblical Literature*
JE	*The Jewish Encyclopedia*, edited by I. Singer et al., 12 vols., New York, 1925
JECS	*Journal of Early Christian Studies*
JEH	*Journal of Ecclesiastical History*
JHS	*Journal of Hellenic Studies*
JJS	*Journal of Jewish Studies*
JQR	*Jewish Quarterly Review*
JRS	*Journal of Roman Studies*
JSJ	*Journal for the Study of Judaism*
JSNT	*Journal for the Study of the New Testament*
JSocSt	*Jewish Social Studies*
JSSR	*Journal for the Scientific Study of Religion*
JTS	*Journal of Theological Studies*
LCL	Loeb Classical Library
MAMA	*Monumenta Asiae Minoris Antiqua*, 8 vols., edited by Sir William M. Calder and J. R. M. Cormack, 1928–65.
MBPF	Münchener Beiträge zur Papyrus-forschung und antiken Rechtsgeschichte
NovTSup	Novum Testamentum Supplements
NTS	*New Testament Studies*
OCPM	Oxford Classical and Philosophical Monographs
OECT	Oxford Early Christian Texts
RAC	*Reallexikon für Antike und Christentum*, edited by Theodor Kluser et al., 1950–
RevQ	*Revue de Qumran*

RGRW	Religions in the Graeco-Roman World
RHR	*Revue de l'histoire des religions*
RRelRes	*Review of Religious Research*
SAOC	Studies in Ancient Oriental Civilization
SBLDS	Society of Biblical Literature Dissertation Series
SecCent	*Second Century*
SJLA	Studies in Judaism in Late Antiquity
SNTSMS	Society for New Testament Studies Monograph Series
StPB	Studia post-biblica
TDNT	*Theological Dictionary of the New Testament,* 10 vols., edited by Gerhard Kittel and Gerhard Friedrich, translated by G. W. Bromiley, 1964–76
TSAJ	Texte und Studien zum antiken Judentum
USQR	*Union Seminary Quarterly Review*
WUNT	Wissenschaftliche Untersuchungen zum Neuen Testament
ZDPV	*Zeitschrift des deutschen Palästina-Vereins*
ZNW	*Zeitschrift für die neutestamentliche Wissenschaft und die Kunde der älteren Kirche*
ZPE	*Zeitschrift für Papyrologie und Epigraphik*

1

SURVEYING THE HORIZON

Background

My attention was first drawn to the phenomenon of apostasy when studying the relation of Jews and Christians in the first two centuries. I was intrigued by passing references to apostates, mostly Jewish, and by the common assertion that they were so rare as to be insignificant. My hunch was that the incidence of apostasy was greater and the assessment of their significance peremptory and, to some extent, defensive. Looking a little further, a number of other things became apparent. We find in the ancient sources, for example, that the accounts of apostasy are almost entirely hostile and unsympathetic. In contrast to the modern world, there are no records of apostates who are proud of and open about their defection or praised by others for removing themselves from the clutches of some fanatical religious group. Ancient people may have done this, but we are not told about it if they did. In addition, the lack of sympathy in ancient sources is often paralleled in modern discussions of them. Scholars, whether consciously or not, tend to take on the viewpoint of their sources on this issue, often no doubt because they write from within the same tradition that they study. Moreover, some of the discussions of apostasy that do exist, especially those few dealing with Christian material, have an essentially theological agenda. They are concerned about the eternal fate of apostates—whether it is inevitable and irrevocable—rather than about apostates as a social phenomenon in the early Christian movement.

This suggests that there is room for taking a look at apostasy as a religious phenomenon of interest in its own right, something worthy of study in a way that is not governed by the perspectives and prejudices of ancient sources. It might even be thought that by looking carefully at how apostates were described and by whom, and by looking at their motives and actions, it is possible with a little imagination to see apostasy from the point of view of the apostate. It is interesting that the experience of conversion, which we might think of as a movement in the opposite direction (i.e., joining rather than leaving), has received considerable attention in studies of the ancient and modern worlds. The two can, of course, be intertwined when a person apostatizes from one group to join another. In this case, someone could be an apostate and a convert at much the same time, and the motives for leaving one group might largely overlap with those for joining another. There is a difference, however, in the way we focus our attention, and in this study it is on the motives for and the process of exiting rather than entering.

The examples I first came across were mostly related to Judaism. It soon became apparent, however, that it would be useful to broaden the enquiry in two ways: first, to include examples of related phenomena in early Christianity and the Greco-Roman world; and second, to take advantage of sociological studies of apostasy in the modern world and the light they may shed on the ancient records. Individual examples from Christian, as from Jewish, sources are sometimes open to more than one interpretation, but few will doubt that we are looking at something that, to a greater or lesser degree, occurred. Analogous examples from the world of Greco-Roman polytheism are more problematic, but I have made the best case for including them that I can. Modern analogies also pose familiar problems related to the considerable social and political differences between ancient and modern societies. However, when they are compared, a surprising number of common themes and broad analogies come to light. I use them only because they are suggestive and because they may alert us to things in the ancient evidence that we may otherwise miss.

The title of the book uses two terms: *apostasy* and *defection*. They, and their cognates, can be used interchangeably. The main difference between them would seem to be that *apostasy (apostate/apostatize)* has acquired a more heavily religious or theological flavor, partly to be found in the ancient sources themselves but partly accrued through its use in polemical conflicts in the later Jewish and Christian traditions. Since we are looking at religious and quasi-religious communities in the ancient world, however, it is entirely appropriate to use it in our discussion as long as we do not allow later accretions to obtrude into or overlay the ancient evidence. Moreover, the Greek term behind *apostasy (apostasis)*, of which the English is simply a transliteration, is used in some of our ancient sources. It is often used broadly of any act of rebellion, but sometimes it is used to describe precisely the phenomenon we wish to isolate. *Defection (defector/defect),* it could be argued, is a more neutral term, sociologically descriptive rather than theologically judgmental, and thus has an advantage over the more freighted alternatives. It does have the advantage of pointing us to a broader spectrum of evidence than we might otherwise consider, that from the pagan world, for example, and it can also encourage us to take a more sympathetic view of apostasy than ancient authors typically encourage.

One way to proceed, therefore, would be to use *apostasy* only when it appears in ancient sources. However, while this would reflect the linguistic whim of ancient writers, it would imply a distinction between phenomena that were in all other respects essentially the same. Another way would be to apply a distinction favored by some sociologists who have studied apostasy in the modern world: a defector is one who leaves, an apostate one who leaves and turns aggressively against the organization he or she has fled.[1] It would be possible to categorize some ancient examples in this way, where the evidence allows, but this would be to override the linguistic nuances of ancient sources where such a distinction is not made. Moreover, not all sociologists favor the distinction, preferring to use apostate as a general term to cover all categories. So it is not easy to find a precise distinction that captures both the phenomenon and the language with which it is described. There

---

1. See the discussion in the concluding chapter.

are advantages to both sets of terms, but I use them interchangeably in what follows, hoping to have learned from the pitfalls of both. Much the same can be said, incidentally, of the terms *heretic* and *dissident*, which will be brought briefly into the discussion below.

In what follows, I rely, with a few exceptions, on evidence up to and just beyond the time of Constantine—including the notorious emperor, Julian the Apostate. This is partly a matter of practicality and convenience, but it also springs from recognition of the dramatic changes that took place after Constantine. The gradual Christianization of the empire—some of it effected by social and political pressures, but much of it increasingly expressed in state and ecclesiastical law—introduced radically new conditions. This did not happen overnight, and we have to wait until at least the fifth century for some of the more rigorous and unbending legislation to appear. But appear it did, and life for pagans—especially the upper classes who had some public presence—became increasingly uncomfortable. As a result, many of them transferred their allegiance to Christianity, some to avoid persecution, some to get ahead, and some no doubt out of genuine conviction. Christians faced a new set of issues too: how to transform state and society in terms of their religious vision; how to cope with their competitors now that they had the upper hand; how to define the version of Christianity that would receive official approval; and how to be sure that conversions were sincere and lasting and not just a matter of convenience. The Jews also found themselves in a topsy-turvy world, as their most intense competitor gained the upper hand. Of course they could convert to the prevailing faith, and if they did so, they were protected from any Jewish backlash by government decree—though some attempt was made to control those suspected of converting for ulterior motives, such as avoiding debt. Yet Jews could not convert, or in some cases even possess, non-Jewish slaves (especially if they were Christians), and intermarriage with Christians was eventually outlawed too. Before Constantine both Jews and Christians had their conflicts with the state, and Christians in particular were subject to official, though often local, persecution. The transformation of the empire after Constantine created a quite different order, one in which the state gradually but inexorably moved toward the imposition of a single religious vision on society that subsumed virtually all areas of life—cult, culture, politics, finances, and law.[2]

The State of the Question

With most topics, the almost obligatory first move is to review the scholarship to date. This can be instructive but also tedious and lengthy. Fortunately, this is not the case with apostasy. There is not very much to survey, which keeps things brief, and what there is usefully alerts us to the difficulties presented by the evidence, the predilections of its interpreters, and the nuances of which we need to be aware. What follows is merely a thumbnail sketch, and many of the issues will be revisited more fully as our discussion proceeds.

A survey of the literature about Jews and Christians in Late Antiquity turns up relatively few discussions of apostasy. This contrasts with fairly frequent discussions of the mirror theme, conversion, on which much has been written. Many writers on Judaism relegate the phenomenon of apostasy to a footnote, mention only the most obvious ostensible examples—such as Tiberius Julius Alexander, the nephew of Philo—and assert without much ado that it was extremely rare.[3] The brief surveys in encyclopedias are sometimes more useful but by definition do not consider the subject in any detail.[4] One or two older discussions of Alexandrian Judaism are more useful and informative.

Wolfson, in his classic study of Philo, has a brief section directly on the theme, and gives a characteristically spirited reading of the social realities that may lie behind the text. Wolfson has no qualms about recognizing that apostasy was a serious problem in Alexandria and that it was different from assimilation to the surrounding culture or even from

---

2. MacMullen (1984:86–101) has an astute discussion of what this meant for pagans and Christians. See also Hillgarth (1986); Karabelias (1994); Brown (2000). For the Jews, see Linder (1987, especially 78–83).

3. For example, Tcherikover (1957.1:37); Hengel (1974.1:31; 2:25n224); Williams (1990:200n22); and Grabbe (1992.2:536–37).

4. Useful encyclopedia articles are found in *JE* 1:12–18; *EncJud* 3:202–15; *EJ* 69–70; *EncTal* 2:404–9.

the casual neglect of Jewish observance by the indifferent (Wolfson 1945.1:73–85). In two early studies, Feldman explored the question of the orthodoxy of the Jews in Egypt during the Hellenistic era and the influence of Hellenistic culture on them. He concluded that while there are undeniable signs of assimilation, they are largely superficial and that there are only a few stray incidents of apostasy. Very few apostates are known by name, and the anti-Semitism that was rife in Alexandria would not have attracted Jews to defect (Feldman 1960; 1986). Later, in his monumental study of Jewish-Gentile interaction in the ancient world, he returned explicitly to the theme of apostasy, only to reinforce his earlier conclusion that it was virtually unknown in Judaism. Most of his discussion is designed to dismiss or deflate the evidence that might point in the other direction (Feldman 1993:65–83). With Feldman one gets the impression that it was important to his concept of Judaism that apostasy should be minimized.

In his book on the origins of Gnosticism, which he locates among disaffected Egyptian Jews in the Hellenistic period, H. Green has a promising subtitle—*Assimilation and Apostasy*—but the subsequent discussion gives little evidence for apostasy and focuses almost entirely on assimilation (Green 1985:155–69). The issue of apostasy in rabbinic literature is briefly taken up by Schiffman in his broader study of Jewish identity in the context of the Jewish-Christian schism (1985). This has now been taken up more fully in Stern's work on the concept of Jewish identity in rabbinic literature (1994:105–12). Both Schiffman and Stern assert that Jewish identity was in some sense indelible, at least in the eyes of the rabbis, so that even though they describe and condemn apostates, they see them as still belonging in some residual way to the community of Jews.

The discussion of Jewish apostasy recently took a considerable leap forward with the appearance of a series of essays by J. G. Barclay (1995a; 1995b; 1998). He constructs a sophisticated grid that attempts to preserve fine distinctions between assimilation, acculturation, and accommodation as ways of reacting to the non-Jewish world and, as a result, makes us think carefully about what we define as apostasy. He also makes creative use of insights from the sociology of deviance and labeling to assess a number of specific instances of defection. Here he insists that there are no absolute measures of apostasy to suit all situations and that it is not an objective state. Apostates are defined less by what they are and do and more by how they are perceived. It is essentially a social process.

The theme of apostasy in early Christian sources has only occasionally been discussed. Sometimes the focus is on theological matters to do with the ultimate fate of the apostate in God's great scheme of things, and in others the issue is discussed solely in relation to the New Testament (Harvey 1985; Marshall 1987).[5] An exception to this is Paul, considered as an apostate from Judaism, who figures in Barclay's various studies and whose defection (or not) has been taken up in a number of recent books. In most of these more recent studies, the discussion rarely extends to other Christian sources, and that is the advantage of two older studies that bear revisiting. Guignebert (1923) explores the evidence for what he calls "demi-Christians" in the ancient church—using literary allusions, epigraphic evidence and the canons of various church councils—and he comes closest to capturing the phenomenon we are interested in. Bardy's work on conversion in the early Christian centuries contains a section on apostasy (1949:294–351) that usefully surveys some of the patristic evidence and concludes with a look at the arch-imperial defector (according to later Christian opinion), Julian the Apostate. His discussion is marred in places by his confusion of heretics with apostates though, as we shall see below, that is in some ways understandable and the distinction is not always an easy one to draw.

I have come across virtually no discussion of the phenomenon of apostasy in connection with the pagan world. It might be thought that this is because the very notion was foreign to the easy-going syncretism of the Greco-Roman world, in which it was not unusual for people to divide their allegiance between a number of deities and cults and where there was little interest in or emphasis upon exclusive commitment to a particular one. That is to some extent true. There were, for example, few strictures on the devotees of one mystery cult participating in another, even if in reality most people did confine their devotion principally to one. Yet there were quasi-religious groups in the ancient world—the philosophical schools, for example—that promoted a strong enough sense of cohesion and commitment that when groups or individuals

---

5. Oropeza (2000) has a good discussion of the theological developments of apostasy and perseverance in the Christian tradition.

split from them it provoked much the same reaction, as Jewish or Christian defectors. Cancik's recent study (1997) of institutions in the ancient world is an attempt to illuminate the Acts of the Apostles, but the evidence he brings to light is far more widely applicable.

If discussions of defection/apostasy are relatively infrequent in modern scholarship, so they are in ancient sources too, and some have concluded from this that the phenomenon itself was rare. It might be argued that, since religious associations (Jewish and Christian at any rate) in the ancient world were more cohesive than they are in our day, their boundaries were more tightly drawn and crossing them was a more obvious, public, and therefore less common, occurrence. But this conclusion may for several reasons be premature. First, groups were as unlikely to publicize tales of defection as they were likely to publicize those of conversion and the resilience of the faithful. Nothing much was to be gained from airing their dirty laundry in public—to outsiders it would be a sign of weakness and to insiders an unfortunate example. Conversions served to enhance their self-image and promote their cause, but defectors undermined them. Eusebius, writing of the persecutions under the emperor Diocletian (284–305 CE), openly admits to this type of filtering. Commenting on those who succumbed during the persecution, including some of the leaders, he says:

> But as to these, it is not our part to describe their melancholy misfortunes in the issue, even as we do not think it proper to hand down to memory their dissensions and unnatural conduct toward one another before the persecution. Therefore we resolved to place on record nothing more about them than what would justify the divine judgment. Accordingly, we determined not even to mention those who have been tried by the persecution, or have made utter shipwreck of their salvation, and of their own free will were plunged in the depths of the billows; but we shall add to the general history only such things as may be profitable, first to ourselves, and then to those that come after us. Let us proceed, therefore, from this point to give a summary description of the sacred conflicts of the martyrs of the divine Word. (Eusebius, *Hist. eccl.* 8.2.2–3)[6]

6. Translations of Eusebius are by Kirsopp Lake (1926).

Eusebius is quite unabashed—he will relate the tales of the glorious martyrs but not of the shameful defectors. Although we do not have as bold a statement from our Jewish sources, one could imagine that the Jews might well have taken the same approach.

Second, it is probable that those who accepted that they were defectors/apostates would normally have preferred not to draw attention to themselves, as has been found to be true in some modern surveys too. Some defectors no doubt carried with them a lingering sense of guilt or did not want to call down the wrath of their community. They saw no need for public renunciation or similar grand gesture but preferred to slip away anonymously into the crowd.

Third, there is no reason in principle to suppose that the boundaries of Jewish, Christian, and pagan communities were always clearly defined. S. J. D. Cohen (1989) has shown, for example, that the evidence for Gentiles attracted to Judaism presents us with a broad spectrum of responses, ranging from simple admiration to full conversion:

- admiring some aspect of Judaism
- acknowledging the power of the God of the Jews
- benefiting or conspicuously befriending the Jews
- practicing some or many rituals of the Jews
- venerating the God of the Jews and denying other gods
- joining the Jewish community, i.e., through slavery or intermarriage
- converting to Judaism and becoming a Jew

The significance of this—and he has good documentation for each category—is the range of responses to and involvement with Judaism. We might expect a similar spectrum of responses as Jews moved in the reverse direction and, in some instances, notably in Alexandria, this appears to have been the case. Defining the range of Jewish reactions to the non-Jewish world is precisely the issue that Barclay explores. There is no reason in principle to think that we cannot make the same assessments for Christians and pagans as well; and in fact, one of the ways I first conceived of this study was to do a Cohen in reverse but expanding it to include Christians and pagans too.

Fourth, I would suggest that while the evidence for defection/apostasy is often allusive and scattered, it is rather more substantial and more significant than is commonly recognized. And, despite the determination of writers like Eusebius to write them out of the record and despite their own inability (or unwillingness) to speak out, they have left their trace, one that is worthy of our attention.

Terms and Concepts

There are limits, as we shall see below, to what terminology alone can tell us. Nevertheless, to look at the way ancient sources describe the phenomenon we are interested in is an essential first step. To help us open up some of the issues, I will introduce discussion of the related term "heresy." This may seem as if we are wandering off at a tangent or trying to explain the obscure by the more obscure, since it is well known that the concept of heresy is itself not entirely transparent. Nevertheless, the two terms are related in our ancient sources, and this is something of which we need to take account. Observing how they overlap and how they differ can help to refine our perception of the human reality underlying them. I do not intend to survey the rise and fall of heresies Jewish, Christian, or otherwise, for that would take us too far afield. I am interested at this point only in the linguistic and conceptual parallels and what we can learn about defining our phenomenon.

One way to open up some of the problems is to start with a statement by the fourth-century Christian historian Eusebius:

> Why are they not ashamed of so calumniating Victor when they know quite well that Victor excommunicated Theodotus the cobbler, the founder and father of this god-denying apostasy *(apostasias)* when he first said that Christ was a real man? For if Victor was so minded towards them as their blasphemy teaches, how could he have thrown out Theodotus who invented this heresy *(haireseos)*? (*Hist. eccl.* 5.28.6, adapted from Lake)

Theodotus, a man with wide intellectual interests and the leader of a group of philosophically inclined Christians who came under the influence of Galen the philosopher and court physician (Walzer

1949:75–86), was also associated with a deviant Christology. The striking thing is that Eusebius, when he describes him, uses "apostasy" and "heresy" as apparent synonyms.[7] These examples do not stand alone. Elsewhere Eusebius writes of Tatian, who abandons *(apostas)* the church after Justin's death and establishes his own doctrine, described as a heresy *(Hist. eccl.* 4.29.3; similarly Irenaeus, *Haer.* 1.28.1), and of Novatian, whose excommunication as the "leader of the heresy" is later described as his "defection *(apostasias)* and schism" *(Hist. eccl.* 6.43.3; 6.45.1). Eusebius reflects a trend that started well before him. Tertullian, for example, generally describes heretics as apostates *(Praescr.* 4.5; 41.6) and specifically labels Valentinus as both *(Val.* 1). Irenaeus sees the followers of Tatian as "heretics and apostates from the truth, patrons of the serpent and of death," and the Gnostics, who for him epitomize heretical belief, as apostates like the serpent in whose footsteps they follow *(Haer.* 3.23.8; 4.1.4).

This provokes a number of questions. Is this usage typical or does it represent the end of a process that was once more complex and discriminating? Had the terms always been used in this way or had they, and the social reality they allude to, once been considered distinct? If the latter, what was the distinction and to whom did it apply? As classic instances of social labeling, did they evolve and operate in the same way? Can we find parallels in Jewish or pagan groups to the things we can observe in the Christian tradition?

What underlies these questions is a simple enough observation. In principle, heretics and apostates could describe two quite different groups: first, those who despite deviant belief or behavior were still considered to be part of a community (dissidents); and second, those who because of deviant belief or behavior were considered to be no longer part of a community (defectors).

At the outset, a number of preliminary observations need to be made. First, a now familiar point: terms like heretic and apostate are rarely self-designations; rather, they are almost always (in the ancient

---

7. The same conjunction of terms is found elsewhere *(Hist. eccl.* 4.29.3–4; 7.7.4). Compare the similar "apostasy" and "schism" [*schismata*] in *Hist. eccl.* 6.45.1; 7.24.6. For *apostasia* meaning "defection" in Eusebius, see also *Hist. eccl.* 3.27.4; 4.23; 4.29.3; *Dem. ev.* 1.7.18; 7.1.117–18; 8.3.18.

world, at least) labels applied to an individual or group by someone
else. Those so labeled, of course, may not see themselves in the same
light at all. This is vividly illustrated by another passage from
Eusebius, where he gives an extract from Dionysius of Alexandria's
letter to Rome:

> For those who came over from the heresies *(haireseon)*, although they
> had abandoned *(apostantas)* the church—or rather, had not aban-
> doned it, but while still reputed members, were charged with fre-
> quenting some false teacher—he [Heraclas] drove from the church.
> *(Hist. eccl.* 7.7.4)

Those whom the bishop thought to have apostatized in fact remained
active in the community and did not see themselves as apostates at
all—at least not until the bishop forced the issue. Thus there is an
important truth in the observation that *heresy* and *apostasy* are terms
that do not transparently describe an objective reality; rather, they are
social labels applied by others (usually, but not always, those in authority) to those with whom they disagreed, as Barclay (1995a) has most
recently pointed out. The perspective of the labeler, it is argued, is thus
all-important and changes from one writer to another, one time to
another and one set of circumstances to another.

Second, while it is clearly important to consider the range and
application of the more obvious linguistic terms *(hairesis, apostasis)* we
need also to distinguish between linguistic usage and social reality. We
cannot assume, in particular, that terms that have become familiar
through long use in a religious tradition were the only ones used to
describe the phenomena we wish to look at. If we restrict ourselves to
linguistic surveys, we will miss a significant portion of the evidence for
dissidence and defection that appears in our sources.

Third, as a sort of extension of the second point and a qualification of the first, we do not necessarily have to be bound by the distinctions—or lack of them—in ancient sources, nor by the perspective
of those who provide them. If, for example, some of them do not
encourage too sharp a dividing line between heretics and apostates,
this needs to be noted, but we should not necessarily be bound by it.
It still seems to me useful to make a distinction between dissidents

who remained within the bounds of a community and defectors who went beyond them, however we label them, though, of course, a person could start as a dissident and end up as a defector. And, while we need to be sensitive to the social dynamics of the process of labeling, not everything is just a matter of perspective. To anticipate material that we shall look at in more detail later, the Antiochene Jew named Antiochus, the Bithynian Christians mentioned by Pliny, and the philosopher Peregrinus seem to me to be unequivocal examples of defection however we look at them. Admittedly, these examples are about as clear-cut as they come, but they do illustrate the point that, to bring some clarity to our own discussion, we may need to impose our own judgment as to who belongs in what category—indeed, as to what the categories are to be!

This points, finally, to a related problem, that of boundaries. What defines the difference between a dissident and a defector, or the moment when an individual passes from one category to the other? This is not easy to answer. It has been argued, for example, that it is difficult to define the taxonomic indicators, the possession of one or more of which signified inclusion in a Jewish or Christian community in the ancient world.[8] It is, by the same token, equally difficult to know which ones have to be absent for an individual to be excluded. The boundaries of Jewish, Christian, and pagan communities would of course have been different, often mutually exclusive, but within each group the boundaries could also be defined differently in different places and at different times. This complicates matters, but not, I think, impossibly.

What then of the terminology itself? Outside Jewish and Christian sources, the primary meaning of *hairesis* was "choice," and its connotation was either neutral or positive but never pejorative. It came to refer to a conviction, point of view, or doctrine and then by extension to different medical and philosophical schools that were often called *haireseis*. More positively it referred to a coherent, articulated doctrine that showed the intellectual talent of its adherents (Sextus Empiricus, *Pyr.* 1.16).[9]

---

8. Smith (1982:1–18).

9. Desjardins (1991). See also Schlier (1964); Brox (1984); Simon (1979); von Staden (1982); and le Boulluec (1985:547).

Competing intellectuals or schools of thought often considered their opponents wrong, but they did not convey this by a pejorative use of *hairesis*. The neutral sense is also found in early Christian and Jewish sources (Acts 5:17; 15:5; 26:5; Josephus, *Ant.* 13.171; 20.199; *War* 2.118; Philo, *Plant.* 151; *Contempl.* 29) and in some later Christian writers (Justin, *Dial.* 17.7; 108.2; *Acts Phil.* 15; Clement, *Stromata* 7.15.89; 7.92.3; Origen, *Cels.* 3.12–13).

What is striking, and as yet without clear explanation, is the shift from a positive or neutral sense to a negative or pejorative one, the more puzzling because both senses can be implied in the same writer. In addition to the neutral uses mentioned above, Acts may contain pejorative uses, when Jews call Christianity a *hairesis* (Acts 24:5,14; 28:22), and Justin certainly does (*1 Apol.* 26:8; *Dial.* 35.3; 51.2; et al.). A transitional sense, on the way from neutral to negative, is implied by 1 Cor 11:18-19 (in connection with *schismata*), Gal 5:20, and 2 Pet 2:1, but it is the context or the accompanying adjectives that convey this. Ignatius, *Trall.* 6:1, in contrast, seems to be an absolute and negative use (and Ignatius, *Eph.* 6:2?). By the early to mid second century, therefore, *hairesis* is established as a technical term for heresy—false teaching or practice, by individuals or groups (mostly gnostic), who are inspired by the devil but whose human ancestry can be traced to particular founding figures (Simon Magus) or to the influence of paganism. This transition can be demonstrated much more readily than its cause. The use of *hairesis* to refer to a doctrine or opinion of a subgroup of Christians is natural enough, but the shift to a largely negative or pejorative sense is not—a problem to which we shall return.

The root meanings of *apostasis/apostateo* (from *aphistemi*) are to "rebel/revolt" or "desert/defect." Mostly the context is political or military, so that in Herodotus and Thucydides *apostasis* often describes a rebellion against a ruler or one-time ally, and it is Josephus's preferred term for referring to the Jewish War.[10] An *apostates* is thus typically a rebel or deserter, though the term can also refer to a fugitive slave or a

---

10. Herodotus, *Hist.* 3.128; 5.113; 7.4; Thucydides 1.75; 3.13 (4x); 5.81; 8.5 (4x); also Polybius 5.57.4; Plutarch, *Cimon* 10 for the verbal form. Josephus uses it in this sense more than sixty times (*War* 1.93; 2.39; 73; *Ant.* 18.118; *Life* 39, 124–25, et al.). In the LXX see 1 Esd 2:27; Neh 2:16; 6:6; 1 Macc 11:14; 13:16; 2 Macc 5:11.

runaway dog.[11] The shift toward the sense we are interested in, defection or desertion without necessarily implying military conflict, can be found in the LXX and Josephus.[12] It is worth noting, however, that most of the interesting examples of defection found in Josephus are described not as "apostatizing" but in more general terms, such as "leaving" or "abandoning" Jewish traditions. Here *kataleipo* is a favorite verb, but it carries this sense only in context and is otherwise too variously used to have a technical sense.[13] Christian use of *apostasis/apostateo*, by contrast, often carries the sense of defection or desertion, to the point where we can consider this the normal meaning in that tradition.[14]

Latin terms convey much the same flavor as the Greek. The most common terms, *defectio/defector* and *desisco,* are used mainly in military or political contexts for groups or individuals who abandon previous alliances or commitments.[15] Pliny uses *desisse/desisto* to describe the Christian deserters in Bithynia, and Cyprian later has a lot to say about those who lapsed *(lapsare)* under the pressure of persecution.[16] Other terms that might have been used—*traitors (traditores)* or *renegades (renegares)*—seem not to occur with any frequency.

11. Plutarch, *Rom.* 9; *Mor.* 821B.

12. *Ant.* 4.129–30; 8.191–92; 16.337; 17.227; *War* 2.634; *Life* 125, 158. An interesting example is *War* 2.467, where the Jews of Scythopolis side with their pagan townsmen against marauding Jews (thus *apostatizing* against their fellow Jews). Fighting ensues, but is not a rebellion in the broader sense. Cf. Philo, *Virt.* 182. In the LXX, see Josh 22:22; 2 Chron 29:19; 33:19; Isa 30:1; Jer 2:19; 1 Macc 2:15; 2 Macc 5:8.

13. *Ant.* 8.190–91; 8.270; 12.240; 12.269; 12.364; 12.384; 18.141. Typically the reference is to Jews who either do (12.240) or do not (12:269) desire to abandon their native laws or forms of worship. Sometimes it is the reverse: Izates' brother, Monobazus, and his relatives, who are impressed by Izates' growing piety and reputation, become eager "to abandon their ancestral religion *(autoi patria katalipontes)* and to adopt the practices *(ethesi)* of the Jews" (20.75).

14. Acts 21:21; 2 Thess 2:3; 1 Tim 4:1; Heb 3:12; *Herm. Vis.* 1.4.2; 2.3.2; 3.7.2; *Sim.* 8.6.4; 8.8.2; 8.8.5; 8.9.1–3; 8.10.3; 9.19.1; Eusebius, *Hist. eccl.* 3.27.4 (Paul's apostasy from Judaism); 5.28.6; 7.24.6; Gregory of Nyssa, *Eun.* 2; Diodorus Siculus, *Bib. Hist.* 21.14.1, 4.

15. *Desisco*: Cicero, *Sest.* 101; *Sull.* 35; Livy 1.27.4; 9.45.6; Tacitus, *Hist.* 1.8; 2.77; Caesar, *Bell. civ.* 1.60.5. *Defectio/defector*: Cicero, *Pis.* 84; *Phil.* 13.39; Caesar, *Bell. gall.* 3.10.2; Tacitus, *Ann.* 4.24; 11.8; 12.50; 16.7; *Hist.* 3.12; Suetonius, *Tib.* 16.1; *Nero* 43.2.

16. Pliny, *Ep.* 96; Cyprian, *De Lapsis* (discussed in chapter 2).

In early Christian sources, *apostasia/apostates* are applied with sufficient regularity to examples of defection that we might think of them as well on the way to becoming technical terms. There are parallels in other sources (Josephus, and particularly the LXX), but they are not used there with the same regularity. Their flavor is largely provided by political and military analogies—the context in which they most frequently occur. Two rather obvious assumptions of ancient usage are also perhaps worth spelling out: first, you can be an *apostates* only when you have had prior association with a group; and second, becoming an *apostates* is a serious act of rebellion, something more than mere dissent or disagreement.

Thus the terms *apostasy* and *heresy* have this in common: in early Christian usage they take on a largely negative sense. In the case of heresy, there is no obvious parallel in Jewish or pagan usage. In the case of apostasy, while there are precedents in Hellenistic Jewish traditions (including the LXX), it is Christians who turn it into a frequent, almost technical term. On the face of it, this suggests that we are dealing with Christian innovation, but before reaching that conclusion, we need to look at possible analogies in the ancient world. The immediate issue is linguistic but broader parallels to the way Christians conceived of and dealt with dissidence and defection are just as interesting.

One place to look for analogies to these Christian developments is in the early rabbinic materials that are roughly contemporaneous. That the two traditions were broadly similar—in their notions of tradition and succession in which heresy is a corruption that disturbs the consensus of the faithful—was argued some while ago by Shaye Cohen.[17] He rather too easily elides the concepts of heresy and apostasy, but his general point stands. Further interesting parallels appear when we look more closely at the rabbinic material. To describe heretics, the rabbis coined a term, *minim*, whose root meaning remains obscure, but whose every use is pejorative. In early rabbinic sources, they are accused of numerous things: healing by sorcery (*t. Ḥul.* 2.22–23), conducting worship in unapproved ways (*m. Meg.* 4.8–9), illegal slaughtering of meat (*m. Ḥul.* 2.9; *t. Ḥul.* 1.1), reading suspect books (*t. Shabb.* 13.5), denying the world to come (*m. Ber.* 9.5), and asserting the existence of two

17. Cohen (1980).

powers in heaven (*m. Meg.* 4.9). *Minim* thus appears to be a fluid concept that could be associated with a number of specific actions or beliefs. The early rabbis are consistent, however, in two things: they pass negative judgment on, and urge avoidance of, the *minim*.[18] Here, as in later traditions, the *minim* are likened to the godless nations (*b. Ḥul.* 41b)—indeed they are sometimes seen to be worse than them (*t. Shabb.* 13.5; *b. Shabb.* 116a; *t. Ḥul.* 1.1; *b. Giṭ.* 45b)—and their ultimate destination is Gehenna (*t. Sanh.* 13.4–5).

The word *'apiqoros* comes to refer to one who deliberately flouts various laws or norms of the community, but it derives from the Greek *Epikouros* (Epicureans) and in tannaitic sources may allude primarily to Sadducees, who were thought to have similar beliefs to the Epicureans (cf. *m. Sanh.* 10.1).[19] The term *anusim* refers in talmudic literature to those who apostatize unwillingly and under pressure, but it does not appear to have been current in this sense in earlier sources. The two most common rabbinic terms for apostates (neither is in the Mishnah) are *mumar* (converted) and *meshummad* (destroyed) and they appear to be interchangeable. One of the earlier definitions of apostates is found in *t. Hor.* 1.5:

> He who eats carrion and non-kosher meat . . . who drinks forbidden (libation) wine, who desecrates the *shabbat,* and who is decircumcised. R. Yose b. Yehuda says, even one who wears a garment of wool and linen. R. Shimeon b. Eleazer adds, even he who commits a transgression for which there is no natural desire.[20]

There is sometimes a hint of a distinction between "limited apostates," who do one of the above, and "comprehensive apostates" who

---

18. See Goodman (1996); Kalmin (1994); and Janowitz (1998). Goodman notes that the paucity and vagueness of early sources on the *minim* may be because the rabbis chose to deal with them by ignoring them. The most detailed summary of rabbinic material on both heresy and apostasy is in Stern (1994:105–12).

19. See Schiffman (1985:43–44); *EncTal* 587–90.

20. Translation from S. Stern (1994:106). This list echoes the misdeeds that, according to the book of *Jubilees,* cause individuals to be rooted out and expelled from Israel: not keeping the sabbath (*Jub.* 2:27–33); eating forbidden foods (6:12); effacing circumcision (15:34); and intermarriage (30:7, 10).

participate in idolatrous worship *(avoda zara)* or were "apostates from the whole Torah," but it is not consistently made (*b. Ḥul.* 4b–5a; *b. Eruv.* 69a–b). Like the *minim*, apostates are considered to be worse than non-Jews and are condemned to eternal punishment in Gehenna (*m. Sheqal.* 1.5; *t. Sanh.* 13.4–5).[21] Certainly they are frequently associated with each other, including in the infamous *birkat ha-minim*, which, like other rabbinic texts, links heretics, apostates, and informers in the same blanket condemnation.[22]

Schiffman (1985:41) once suggested the following distinction: heretics diverge from the established religion in their beliefs, apostates in their actions. But rabbinic traditions—where, as we have seen, the *minim* are condemned as much for deviant actions as for false belief—do not support him. It may be that "in some respects the *minim* are no more than a variety of apostates" (Stern 1994:111), but only in some respects. Certainly, heretics and apostates are equally roundly condemned and assigned the same ultimate fate. Apostates appear to be distinguished, however, by their more flagrant deviation from Jewish traditions (see *t. Hor.* 1.5 above), most commonly worship of *avoda zara* in some form or another, and they are usually condemned for breaches of halakha and not matters of belief.[23] Indeed, for the rabbis, one of the problems with the *minim* was precisely that they did not stand out but looked in many respects just like other Jews. And there is a further crucial difference: apostates in general were judged to have abandoned the covenant community, while

---

21. This summary on *mumar* and *meshummad* is taken from Stern (1994:106–7), including the translation of *t. Hor.* 1.5. See also Schiffman (1985:41–49). In Amoraic sources, a distinction is made between apostates out of convenience (following forbidden desires) and apostates out of conviction (spite) (*b. Avod. Zar.* 26b; *b. Hor.* 11a). *Mumar* may have been substituted for *meshummad* in the printed texts by censors—some of whom were converted Jews—who did not like the nuances of *meshummad*. So Zeitlin (1963–64:84–86).

22. See the texts collected in Horbury (1982:43–44).

23. Although *t. Ḥul.* 1.1 implies that some of the *minim* were suspected of idolatrous worship (*avoda zara*, Stern 1994:110). Stern thinks that *minim* were thought worse than ordinary apostates but provides little evidence for this (1994:111). He also states that the term *meshummad* usually refers to comprehensive apostates, not the ordinary apostates who merely transgress one command (106).

heretics, however troublesome, remained within it (*Sifra Nedabah* parasha 2:3 on Lev 1:2).[24]

Rabbinic and Christian traditions are in some ways similar: they both develop the concepts of heresy and apostasy and describe them with separate terms (in either Greek or Hebrew); and, apart from the nonpejorative (and mostly early) use of *hairesis* in Christian sources, they both come to understand the terms and the phenomena they refer to in a negative way. In rabbinic sources, however, the distinction between heretics and apostates is more consistently preserved, even if they are often accused of the same things and equally condemned. Heretics and apostates are two different species, not two ways of talking about the same species. In interesting ways, the traditions run parallel, but they are not identical. Is it likely that they interacted with and influenced each other? Not much encourages such a view. The use of different languages would have been one barrier, and there is little to suggest that Christians were in general well informed about developments within rabbinic Judaism. The rabbinic movement was itself somewhat insular, and it was not for several centuries that the rabbinic leaders were able to exert widespread control over Jewish communities. There may have been parallel developments in diaspora Judaism, but this we do not know.[25] Perhaps the similarities arise simply because they are similar sorts of tradition.[26] We cannot rule out cross-fertilization, but not much points in this direction.

In one of the more extensive discussions of pagan evidence, Norbert Brox concludes that any attempt to find Greco-Roman parallels to the

24. For a translation of the Sifra passage, see Sanders (1977:84). Stern defines (rabbinic) apostates as in almost all respects the reverse of proselytes, except that proselytes lose their previous identity and apostates theoretically retain theirs (in this life) (1994:109). See the discussion on apostates and Jewish identity in the concluding chapter below.

25. Desjardins (1991:76–77) suggests that the use by Jews of *hairesis* to refer to Christians (Acts 24:5; 28:22; Justin *Dial.* 17.1; 108.2) may reflect early Jewish usage. But not all of these are necessarily negative, and they may at any rate only witness to Christian usage placed on Jewish lips.

26. Cohen (1980:6). He notes that both are book religions, in which doctrines of tradition and succession are inevitable; and that both espouse a form of monotheism, which encourages notions of unity, oneness, and exclusivity.

Christian concept of heresy founders on two obstacles: that disputes and disagreements roughly analogous to those in the churches (e.g., in the philosophical schools) do not affect the semantic field of *hairesis* in pagan sources; and that the influence of such disputes on Christian concepts of deviation can only be surmised, because there is no instance where we can, as it were, observe it actually occurring.[27] He also notes that the absence of normative beliefs and confessional orthodoxy in the schools, as well as the introduction of the concept of revelation as the source of divine truth in the churches, placed them in radically different worlds. His linguistic point seems correct.[28] However, the contrast in concepts of orthodoxy and revelation is overdrawn and somewhat abstract, and at any rate applies only to the later Christian period when such ideas took hold. Moreover, his focus on linguistic usage tends to override other kinds of pertinent evidence.

In contrast, Shaye Cohen has suggested that the historiographical outlook of the philosophical schools—the pristine teachings of the founder, their transmission through a chain of tradition, the splits and rivalries—may well have influenced both the Jewish (rabbinic) and Christian ideas of heresy.[29] More recently, Cancik has argued that the true analogies for what he calls Luke's "institutional history" are the philosophical schools, with their disputes over unity, inheritance, and continuity (1997). The point of contrast for Cancik is with Greco-Roman religion, in which he finds no such analogy. He focuses on Acts, but quite apart from the observation that Acts is in many ways the precursor of later concepts of Christian orthodoxy and historiography, much of the evidence he collects can be applied more generally to the issue we are looking at. Cancik provides a rich array of examples that can be used to flesh out Cohen's proposal.[30] There are many instances of disagreement and lively polemic both between and within the

27. Brox (1984:248–59).

28. A check through *TLG* of the use of *hairesis* in a large range of classical writers turned up no parallels to the negative Christian usage.

29. Cohen (1980:6–8).

30. Loveday Alexander's perceptive comments (1994) on the parallels between Christian groups and philosophical and medical schools do not deal directly with the issue that concerns us. Medical schools are an important point of comparison too, but there is less information about their rifts—see von Staden (1982:76–110).

Hellenistic schools. To anticipate again material that we shall look at more fully later, there was the famous schism within the Platonic Academy under Antiochus of Ascalon (died 68 BCE), and there were people like Menedemus, who founded new schools but within the same tradition. Equally interesting are those who move from one school or system of thought to another, like Aristo of Alexandria and Cratippus of Pergamum, both of whom were said to have "defected from the Academy" *(apostatesantes tes Akademeias)* when Aristus, Antiochus's brother, took over the reins.[31] This striking use of *apostatesantes* reminds us of Dionysus of Heraclea ("the renegade"), who abandoned Zeno the Stoic *(apostas de tou Zenon)* and became a hedonist (Diog. L. 7.166–67), and of Chrysippus, who separated himself *(apeste)* from Cleanthes (Diog. L. 7.179).

A number of things are worth noting. First, we have evidence of internal divisions within a school, transfer of allegiance from one school to another, and perhaps abandonment of philosophy altogether. Associated with this are bitter exchanges, counterattacks by those who have been abandoned, and endless squabbles over inheritance of the true tradition. Second, while not exactly a technical term, *apostateo* is fairly regularly used to describe defection from one school to another or even from philosophy altogether. Thus, although the negative use of *hairesis* is not found, the negative use of *apostateo* is. And although there is no linguistic distinction between dissidents and defectors, both sorts of behavior can be found in the records. Thus the analogy with the philosophical schools works well, at least for some of the features we are interested in, and this will be a promising lead to follow later in our discussion.

Consideration of the linguistic evidence does not in itself resolve all the problems of definition. There is something inherently arbitrary and indeterminate in the concept of apostasy/defection. For one thing, while in the modern world some people might describe themselves as a defector, or a heretic, generally in the ancient world such labels appear to be applied by others. Those so labeled, of course, might not

---

31. The quotation is from the *Ind. Acad.* col. 35 (not available to me), as found in Cancik (1997:691), and the evidence for Menedemus is in *Ind. Acad.* col. 6. Cancik discusses several other examples of inter- and intra-school competition (686–95).

see themselves at all in the same light. In all these cases, therefore, the terms have no clear or definitive sense except from the point of view of the labeler.

It seems that some ancient sources do not encourage too sharp a dividing line between heretics and apostates. This needs to be noted, but we should not necessarily be bound by it. It still seems to me useful to make a distinction between dissidents who remained within the bounds of a community and defectors who strayed beyond them. However we label them, though, of course, a person could start as a dissident and end up as an apostate. We may have to ignore the judgments of ancient writers about the status of those they oppose and the labels they use to describe them in order to set limits, and bring some clarity, to our own discussion.

Some of these issues about definitions will be revisited, but for now I shall use *defector* and *apostate* to describe those who considered themselves, or were considered by others, to have abandoned the main practices and/or beliefs of their religious community, in extreme cases even turning against it. They are thus unlike dissidents, who can be seen as wayward members of the community but members nonetheless. And, while various degrees of assimilation to the surrounding culture may be possible without defection, apostates can be considered to be those whose assimilationist tendencies finally took them beyond the limits of their community.

2

JEWISH APOSTATES

Literary Evidence

The issue of apostasy is raised in dramatic, and for later generations archetypal, form at the beginning of our period in the events surrounding the Maccabean rebellion, starting ca. 168 BCE. The simplest version is found in 1 Maccabees:

> Then the king wrote to his whole kingdom that all should be one people; and that all should give up their particular customs. All the Gentiles accepted the command of the king. Many even from Israel gladly adopted his religion; they sacrificed to idols and profaned the sabbath. (1 Macc 1:41-43)

> He appointed inspectors over the whole people and commanded the towns of Judah to offer sacrifice town by town. Many of the people, all those who forsook the law, joined them, and they did evil in the land. (1 Macc 1:51-52)

What precipitated the attempt by the Seleucid king Antiochus IV to suppress the practice of Judaism, the course of events that led up to it, the extent to which he was egged on by Jewish factions in Jerusalem, and the different ambitions of Jewish leaders such as Jason and Menelaus are all matters that are still the subject of considerable debate.[1] It is generally agreed that 1 and 2 Maccabees reflect the views of the Jewish dynasty founded by the rebels who successfully resisted Antiochus and that their accounts may be overly simplified. However, some things are fairly certain: first, that there were attempts to reform and, finally, to suppress Judaism; second, that Jewish reaction was mixed, some succumbing to and others resisting Antiochus's decrees. Thus it appears there were two kinds of apostate: those who supported Hellenization and the reform of Judaism, some supporting the prom- ulgation of the decrees that outlawed Judaism and enforced the wor- ship of foreign gods; and those who succumbed during the persecution that ensued. The latter were reacting to a deadly rule of terror (1 Macc 1:50), some willingly (1 Macc 1:43) but most presumably not. They were the victims of circumstance, of "those enforcing the apostasy" (*hoi katanagkazontes ten apostasian*, 1 Macc 2:15).

The other group, led by Menelaus, appears to have colluded with Antiochus both in the initial transformation of Jerusalem into a Hellenistic city and in the subsequent suppression of Judaism (2 Macc 5:8, 15). Josephus, writing in the first century CE, typically describes them as follows:

> The populace was divided between the two, the Tobiads being on the side of Menelaus, while the majority of the people supported Jason; and being hard pressed by him, Menelaus and the Tobiads withdrew, and going to Antiochus informed him that they wished to abandon their country's laws *(patrious vomous katalipontes)* and the way of life prescribed by these, and to follow the king's laws and adopt the Greek way of life. (Josephus, *Ant.* 12.240)[2]

The verb "abandon" *(kataleipo/katalyo)* is favored in Josephus's account, and the object is usually ancestral laws or ancestral worship *(patrioi*

---

1. Grabbe (1992.1:221–84) has an excellent summary.

2. Translations of Josephus are from the Loeb Classical Library edition unless otherwise indicated.

nomoi/patria threskeia; cf. *Ant.* 12.269, 364, 384–85).[3] The hostile and simplified accounts that have come down to us give little insight into their motives. Internecine struggles, greed, and the lust for power may all have played their part, but we should not dismiss the role of genuine conviction. That is, these Jews were probably convinced that Judaism in its traditional form was passé and that the future lay with the broader and more cosmopolitan ideals of Hellenization. Some (e.g., Jason) may have thought in terms of transforming Judaism in response to powerful cultural trends, somewhat like the Jews who tried to modernize Judaism in the nineteenth century.[4] But others appeared to have effectively placed themselves outside the community by encouraging the abolition of all the traditional expressions of Jewish allegiance and identity.

In a later Maccabean work written in the first century CE, a similarly oppressive situation is described that put the Jews of Alexandria under the gun.

> He [Philopator] erected a pillar on the tower at the palace and inscribed on it, "That none of those who did not sacrifice should be allowed to enter their temples, and that all Jews should be required to enroll in the census and be reduced to the condition of slaves, and that any who spoke against it should be taken by force and put to death, that those who were enrolled should be branded by fire on their bodies with an ivy leaf, the emblem of Dionysus, and should be registered according to their former restricted status." But so as not to appear to be an enemy to them all he added, "But if any of them prefer to join those who are initiated into the mysteries, they would be on the same footing as the citizens of Alexandria." Some who objected strongly to the price that the city had to pay for the practice of its religion surrendered gladly, expecting to participate in some of the prestige that would come from being associated with the king. But most resisted with gallantry of spirit and did not abandon their religious practice. (3 Macc 2:28-32)

3. Josephus, *Ant.* 20.75, uses the same language to describe King Izates' abandonment *(katalipontes)* of his ancestral religion and adoption of Judaism.

4. I say "somewhat like" because it is easy to romanticize the Jewish Hellenizers in terms of nineteenth-century Reform Judaism, as does Bickerman (1975).

... that those of the Jewish people who had wittingly transgressed against God and his Law should receive the due punishment at their hands, stressing that those who had transgressed the divine commandments for their belly's sake would never be well disposed to the king's business either. The king acknowledged the truth of what they said and, praising them, granted them full indemnity to destroy ... those who had transgressed the Law of God. (3 Macc 7:10-12)[5]

Ptolemy IV Philopator, according to the narrative, had initially been affronted when he was refused entry into the Jerusalem Temple. In the ensuing persecution some Jews accepted initiation into the Dionysiac mysteries and Alexandrian citizenship rather than humiliation and death. For this they were despised and ostracized by their fellow Jews. Later the king absolved the Jews of any wrongdoing, blaming his earlier policies on misinformation. Restoring the Jews to their former status, he also gave permission for the defectors, numbering three hundred according to 3 Macc 7:15, to be hunted down and put to death. Ostensibly the events took place in Philopator's reign (222–203 BCE), but it is more likely that traditional material (some of it perhaps stemming from Philopator's time) has been adapted to respond to a later crisis under Roman rule. In general terms, the combination of an assault on the Jerusalem Temple together with the persecution of Alexandrian Jewry suggests a date during the reign of Gaius Caligula (38–41 CE).[6] Caligula's dramatic threat to erect his statue in the Jerusalem Temple and the flare-up during his rule over Jewish religious and civic rights in Alexandria provide a plausible context for the sort of crisis alluded to in 3 Maccabees. The author is not averse to foreign rule per se and sees no conflict between commitment to Jewish practice and respect for Gentile rule. He opposes only those who threaten Jewish identity—rulers who run amok and Jews who defect. The defectors seemed to have acted out of fear, a desire to enhance their reputation

5. Translations by H. Anderson in Charlesworth (1985).

6. Collins (1983:104–11) gives strong arguments for this dating. He notes that the fit with events in Alexandria during Caligula's reign is loose, more like the account of Philo in *Legatio ad Gaium* than what is known from other sources. On Caligula and the Jews, see Grabbe (1992.2:401–11).

with the king (2:31) and, more obscurely, "for their belly's sake" (7:11). This is not very helpful in getting at their motives, but the overall implication is that they were responding to external pressure but also acting out of self-interest. What they gained (temporarily) was Alexandrian citizenship, but only at the price of apostasy and the loss of solidarity with their fellow Jews. There is no corroborating account of these defectors and their subsequent fate at the hands of their fellow Jews, but even if some of the details are legendary, there is no reason to suppose that Jewish defectors existed only in the author's imagination. The problem may well have been real and the use of traditional stories an oblique way of addressing it.

A similarly radical incidence of apostasy is recorded by Josephus. Following a description of the growth and influence of the Jewish colony in Antioch and the attraction of non-Jews to their ceremonies, he describes the following incident at the beginning of the Jewish War:

> Now just at the time when war had been declared and Vespasian had recently landed in Syria, and when hatred of the Jews was everywhere at its height, a certain Antiochus, one of their number and highly respected for the sake of his father, who was chief magistrate of the Jews in Antioch, entered the theatre during an assembly of the people and denounced *(enedeiknyto)* his own father and the other Jews, accusing them of a design to burn the whole city to the ground in one night; he also delivered up some foreign Jews as accomplices to the plot. On hearing this, the people, in uncontrollable fury, ordered the men who had been delivered up to be instantly consigned to the flames. And all were forthwith burnt to death in the theatre. Then they rushed for the Jewish masses, believing the salvation of their native place to be dependent on their prompt chastisement. Antiochus inflamed their fury; for, thinking to furnish proof of his conversion *(metabole)* and of his detestation of Jewish customs by sacrificing after the manner of the Greeks, he recommended that the rest should be compelled to do the same, as the conspirators would thus be exposed by their refusal. This test being applied by the Antiochenes, a few submitted and the recalcitrants were massacred. Antiochus, having next procured the aid of troops from the Roman general, domineered with severity over his fellow Jewish citizens, not

permitting them to repose on the seventh day, but compelling them to do everything exactly as on other days; and so strictly was the weekly day of rest abolished, but the example having been started there spread for a short time to the other cities as well. (*War* 7.47–53)

This extraordinarily vivid account is not unlike the Maccabean situation: Jews are required to abandon their traditions and participate in foreign cults at the instigation of renegade members of their own community. Some Jews were forced to apostatize under severe pressure, but one, at least, did so willingly. The difference lies in Antiochus's sudden, unexplained and radical shift of allegiance. Unlike Menelaus, he does not appear to have been mixed up in national politics or subjected to the political machinations of foreign overlords. We are told only that he was the son of a prominent Antiochene Jew, whom he denounced along with all the others, and that his "conversion" (i.e., defection) took place when Jews were hated everywhere. While rebellion against one's parents is not unknown as a cause of defection—a means of signaling independence and throwing over the traces—we can never know what tensions and frustrations may have provoked Antiochus to turn against his father. More significant, perhaps, was the hostility toward the Jews and their unstable political standing. Maybe he was convinced that the Jews were doomed, especially once they had challenged the might of Rome, and feared that he would go down with them. At any rate, he fits an observable pattern in apostates down through the centuries: many of them became the most hostile and vociferous opponents of the tradition that they had only recently abandoned.

Not all forms of social and political pressure are associated with a crisis. In 3 Macc 1:3 there is mention of Dositheus, a Jewish servant of the king, "who had renounced the Law and abandoned his ancestral traditions" *(metabalon ta nomima kai ton patrion dogmaton apellotri-omenos)*. When and for what reason we are not told, but since he appears to have been well placed in the court of a foreign ruler, we may not go far wrong in supposing that social and political ambitions lay at the root of it. Traditional commitments were more than outweighed by the prospect of influence and advancement in the corridors of power. This Dositheus appears to be the same one described in a papyrus as a scribe in the court of Ptolemy Euergetes I and "the priest of Alexander and the gods Adelphoi and the gods Euergetai" (*CPJ* 127).[7] Appointment as priest of a cult centered on Alexander and the deified Ptolemies in Alexandria was scarcely compatible with continued commitment to the Jewish way of life, at least from a Jewish point of view (including that of the author of 3 Maccabees). This may be a snippet of tradition that is included for historical reasons and has no immediate reference to the situation at the time of writing. But if, as discussed above, 3 Maccabees deliberately uses traditions to encode messages for the present, the allusion might be to those who colluded willingly with Roman rule. Dositheus, the model of a successful defector, might even have been an example to those other Jews who were tempted to defect when the heat was on. Similarly, pursuit of a political career and submission to social pressures may also have led to the deracination of Herod's great-grand-children, who were brought up in Rome and abandoned *(ekleipo)* Jewish customs in favor of a Greek way of life (*Ant.* 18.141). They are also examples of the importance of upbringing in preserving attachment to ancestral customs.

A more notorious instance of the combination of social assimilation and political ambition is Philo's nephew, Tiberius Julius Alexander. He is an important and, for the discussion of Jewish apostasy, a pivotal figure. This is partly because we know more about him than we do about others, who are either anonymous or dismissed with a cursory line, and partly because Josephus makes a specific accusation about him:

> . . . Tiberius Alexander, the son of that Alexander who had been alabarch in Alexandria and who surpassed all his fellow citizens both in ancestry and in wealth. He was also superior to his son Alexander in his religious devotion *(pros ton theon eusebeia)*, for the latter did not continue in the customs of his forefathers *(tois gar patriois ouk enemeinen houtos ethesin)*. (*Ant.* 20.100)

Josephus's statement has been read in different ways, as have the various stages of Alexander's career. He was born into one of the wealthiest, best-connected, and influential families in Alexandria, and this alone would have exposed him regularly to the culture and routines of the

---

7. Barclay (1998:83–84); Modrzejewski (1993:83–85).

pagan aristocracy. He was almost certainly educated in a Greek gymnasium, a common training for military officers and, in some periods, a favored route to advancement for wealthy Alexandrian Jews. A gymnasium education involved serious compromises for Jews, and Philo condemns those who used education for social advancement (*Leg.* 3.164–65) or socioeconomic mobility (*Spec.* 2.18–19).[8]

The surviving fragments of Philo's *De Providentia* record a discussion about the problem of divine providence between Philo and a man called Alexander. Many identify this Alexander with Philo's nephew when he was a young man: "This Alexander may be taken with fair certainty to be Philo's nephew Alexander Tiberius, who later apostatized from Judaism."[9] In the debate, Alexander is attributed with doubts about and arguments against divine providence on the grounds that the wicked prosper and the righteous suffer—the abiding and still unresolved problem of theodicy—while Philo makes the case for holding to the notion of divine control of the world. If Philo's interlocutor is correctly identified, we may suppose that, like others Philo mentions, his nephew had some philosophical problems with Judaism.

Most fully reported is Tiberius Alexander's immensely successful military career, including two spells in Egypt (as military commander of Upper Egypt in the 40s, and prefect of Egypt in the 60s) and two in Judea (as procurator in 46–48 and second-in-command to Titus at the end of the Jewish War). He dealt harshly with rebellious Jews in both Judea and Egypt. When procurator of Judea, he had the rebel sons of Judas the Galilean crucified (Josephus, *Ant.* 10.100–103); after mediation failed, he suppressed Jewish troublemakers in Alexandria (Josephus, *War* 2.487–98); and he was on Titus's staff during the final siege of Jerusalem in 70 CE, when he voted (with Titus) not to raze the Temple (Josephus, *War* 6.237–43). In 69 CE he declared for the Roman general Vespasian as emperor and may, as a consequence, have been rewarded with the post of prefect of the praetorian guard in Rome,

8. Wolfson (1947.1:79) thought that Jews did not attend the gymnasia, but the evidence points in the other direction. Nor is there convincing evidence for Jewish gymnasia in Alexandria. See Feldman (1960:222–26) and Sandelin (1991:112–13, 138–42).

9. Colson (1985:447). Some think it is the same Alexander as in Philo's *Animabalis*. Hadas-Lebel (1973:23, 46) is not sure that Alexander is, in either case, Philo's nephew.

though there is some doubt about the evidence for this (Turner 1954:61–64).

Was he an apostate? Josephus does not precisely say this, and Etienne (2000) has argued that none of the evidence necessarily points in this direction and that he should be given the benefit of the doubt. He notes, first, that loose adherence to or lack of respect for Jewish customs does not amount to apostasy. That precise accusation, which Etienne thinks must involve a deliberate decision to abandon Judaism and/or join a pagan cult, is not made by Josephus. As I noted in the opening chapter, however, Josephus favors phrases like "abandoning/not continuing in the customs" rather than a technical use of *apostates* or some such to describe defectors, so not too much rests on the absence of a single term.[10] Attending a gymnasium or otherwise taking part in Hellenisitic cultural events must have involved some compromises, but it did not necessarily lead to abandonment of one's Jewish heritage, as the case of Philo clearly shows.[11] That the doubts expressed in *De Providentia,* if correctly attributed to Alexander, express intellectual uncertainty but do not in themselves amount to apostasy, is true; but if there are other reasons to suspect him of turning away from Judaism, they may be used to shed some light on Alexander's thinking in his formative years. It is worth noting that Tiberius Alexander probably began his career as a Roman official at the time his father was freed by Claudius, when he succeeded Gaius Caligula as emperor (Turner 1954:58). This would have left him well disposed to the emperor from the start. His actions against fellow Jews, Etienne rightly notes, could have been motivated by political necessity rather than religious disenchantment. They would be consistent with, but not prove, a drift away from Judaism.

More significant is the inevitable contact with pagan religion that must have come with his administrative and military roles in the

10. Note the similarity between Tiberius "not remaining in *(diemeinen)* the customs" and the proselytes who do "remain" *(emeinan)* as distinct from those who "leave" *(apestesan)* in *Ag. Ap.* 2.123.

11. See further Kerkeslager (1997) for the case of a Hellenized Jew who participates in a theatrical mime, but in a way that only accentuates his Jewishness by virtue of his circumcised penis.

empire. His military career and any ambitions he harbored depended on absorption into the military ethos. Part of his routine military and political duties would have involved participation in civic cults—when he was prefect of Egypt, for example—and there is evidence of him dedicating a relief to the emperor and pagan deities (Turner 1954:56–57). Etienne underplays this by arguing that contact with, even participation in, pagan religious rites (which he admits would have been unavoidable in a military career) may show little or no respect for Jewish customs but do not signify a rupture with Judaism. But in a culture that emphasized praxis as a primary expression of religious adherence and that had a deep horror of contamination by pagan cults, this kind of distinction would have made little sense.

It is in my view significant that Josephus makes a clear distinction between Alexander and his father, a man who also had an important administrative role in Alexandria and was equally exposed to the attractions of pagan life. The one remained committed to Jewish ways, the other did not. That is, the distinction is deliberate and pointed and not just a throwaway line. Josephus also describes Alexander Tiberius's attitude toward Judaism in language that he uses elsewhere to describe defectors. That he describes him this way only in *Antiquities* and not in *Jewish War* is best explained by noting that the latter was published when Alexander was still a figure of stature and influence, and the former in the 90s of the first century when he was freer to express his real opinion (Turner 1954:52; Barclay 1995a:120). Also, Josephus's positive experience with the Romans after he surrendered during the war and allied himself with them might naturally have made him positively disposed to a fellow Jew who went a similar route. That he was not suggests that he had some grounds for his judgment.

Is it enough then to say that Tiberius Alexander, "if not actually a renegade, was at least a studious neglecter of Judaism"?[12] Though we do not have his view on the matter, to describe him merely as an unobservant Jew seems not to catch the flavor of his career, and if he did not

---

12. Applebaum (1976:705); contra Feldman (1993:81). Barclay (1995a:120) raises the interesting hypothetical question whether Alexander would have been viewed differently if he had been able to advantage the Jews in Egypt and Judea. We can only guess.

renounce Judaism, he appears to have followed a career that steadily drew him toward the practices, ideals, and politics of the non-Jewish world. I suspect that the various things we can glean about him point cumulatively to someone who was, to all intents and purposes, a defector. The factors that led to his gradual deracination can be surmised as follows: Greek education, philosophical doubts, worldly ambition, military responsibilities, and family gratitude.

A rich source of information for run-of-the-mill forms of defection is to be found in the two prominent Jewish writers Josephus and Philo. By "run-of-the-mill" I mean defections that occur not in response to extreme political crises but more gradually and, some would say, insidiously as part of the process of accommodation and assimilation to the non-Jewish world. That Josephus was concerned about contemporary problems of Jewish assimilation and apostasy is indicated by the way he recasts two biblical narratives. The first is the story in Numbers 25 of the seduction of Israelite men by the Midianite and Moabite women that led to the eating of forbidden foods, worship of foreign gods, murder of an apostate Jew (Zimri = Zambrias in Josephus) and his pagan consort by the zealous Phinehas, and further punishment of Israel by a plague (Josephus, *Ant.* 4.126–55). Josephus's version involves considerable expansion of the biblical story (compare Philo's modest retelling of the same story in *Mos.* 1.294–304), and it centers on the malign link between unchastity/intermarriage and idolatry/apostasy. Zambrias, who openly takes a pagan wife and sacrifices to a plurality of gods, is allowed a vigorous speech by Josephus that gives what W. C. van Unnik has called a "rationale for apostasy."[13]

> Zambrias said: "You, Moses, keep the laws on which you have bestowed your care, having secured confirmation of them only through these men's simplicity; for, if they were not men of that character, you would have learned before now through divine punishment that Hebrews are not duped so easily. But you will not get me to follow your tyrannical orders; for you have done nothing up to

---

13. Van Unnik (1974:261). In this paragraph I am merely summarizing van Unnik. He is followed by Borgen (1995:33–36). The pressure on Jews to join in pagan worship is indicated in Josephus, *Ant.* 12.125–26; 16.58–59; *Ag. Ap.* 2.66.

now except by wicked artifice, under the pretext of "laws" and "God," to create servitude for us and sovereignty for yourself, robbing us of life's pleasures and of that independence of action *(autexousion)* which belongs to free men who have no master. . . . It is you who deserves punishment for having decided to abolish things which all the world has unanimously confessed to be excellent and for having established, against universal opinion, your own falsehoods. . . . I have married a foreign wife. . . . And I sacrifice to gods to whom I hold sacrifice to be due, thinking it right to get at the truth from many persons, and not live as under the tyranny, hanging all my hopes on one. *(Ant.* 4.145–49; LCL adapted)

Moses is attacked as a despot who subjected the Jews to servitude, imposed legislation that runs counter to that of the rest of the world, deprived them of their independence and freedom, and banned them from the worship of a plurality of gods that many other peoples enjoyed. It is a radical attack on Jewish particularity and exclusiveness and a defense of pluralism and polytheism. It draws on themes familiar in ancient debates and no doubt seductive to some Jews—the desire for independence *(autexousian)* and the value of widely shared opinion *(argumentum e consensu omnium)*. The extent of Josephus's changes to and expansion of the biblical underlay encourages us to think he has rewritten the biblical story with contemporary problems in mind. The arguments used by Zambrias may very well reflect the views of Jewish defectors who had succumbed to intellectual arguments in favor of the pluralism of the pagan world, while at the same time Josephus warns his fellow Jews of the ease with which transgression of food laws and intermarriage can lead down the slippery slope to apostasy (a theme that Philo harps on too).

The revisions to and expansion of the story of Solomon's downfall (1 Kgs 11:1-13; Josephus, *Ant.* 8.190–98) have been interpreted along the same lines.

He did not persevere in this way until his death, but abandoned *(katalipon)* the observance of his fathers' customs and came to an unexpected end based on what we have previously said about him. For he became madly enamored of women and indulged in excesses of passion; not satisfied with the women of his own country he married many from foreign nations as well . . . thereby transgressing the laws of Moses who forbade marriage with persons of other races, and began to worship their gods to gratify his wives and his passion for them—which is the very thing the lawgiver foresaw when he warned the Hebrews against marrying women of other countries lest they might be entangled with foreign customs and fall away from those of their fathers and worship the gods of these women and neglect to honor their own god. (*Ant.* 7.190–93)

In his dotage, Solomon decides to take several foreign wives and becomes so besotted with them that he begins to worship their gods and oversees the construction of idolatrous images. Josephus treats him with some sympathy and attenuates his guilt with reference to his senility, but he is still roundly condemned as a traitor to his father and his people. For Jewish readers "the story dramatically highlights the ongoing contemporary problem of assimilation vis-à-vis fidelity to 'ancestral customs.'"[14]

A similar problem presumably affected proselytes too. Even though they had made a difficult choice in joining the Jewish community, and are expansively praised by Philo for it (see below), not all of them stayed on. Josephus (*Ag. Ap.* 2.123) tells us specifically that "many of them [Greeks] have agreed to adopt our laws; of whom some have remained *(emeinan)* faithful, while others, lacking the necessary endurance, have again seceded *(hoi ten karterian ouch hypomeinantes palin apestesan)*." A specific but unusual example is Polemo, the king of Cilicia, who got circumcised in order to marry Berenice, but when he was abandoned by her he in turn abandoned Judaism (Josephus, *Ant.* 20.145–46). While Josephus, like Philo, was proud of Gentile converts, he admits that not all of them lasted the course. The implication is that for some converts life in the Jewish community was too demanding— a judgment that is of course Josephus's and, even if accurate, could cover a lot of things. One difference between these and other defectors is that these presumably returned to a life they had already known. The

14. Begg (1997:313). Van Unnik (1974:251) also connects this story with Josephus's account of Numbers 25.

pull was not to the other so much as to the familiar—defection as reversion.

Philo is a rich source of information about Jews who drifted away from their community:

> The proselytes become at once temperate, continent, modest, gentle, kind, humane, serious, just, high-minded, truth lovers, immune to the desire for money and pleasure; just as conversely the rebels from the holy laws *(tous ton hieron nomon apostantes)* are seen to be incontinent, shameless, unjust, frivolous, petty-minded, quarrelsome, friends of falsehood and perjury, who have sold their freedom *(eleutheria)* for delicacies, strong liquor, sweetmeats and the enjoyment of another's beauty *(eumorphias),* thus ministering to the delights of the belly and the organs below it—delights which end in the gravest injuries to body and soul. (*Virt.* 182)[15]

> The proselyte exalted aloft by his happy lot will be gazed at from all sides, marvelled at and held blessed by all for two things of highest excellence: that he came over to the camp of God and that he has won a prize best suited to his merits, place in heaven firmly fixed, greater than words dare describe. While the nobly born who has debased the coinage of his noble birth *(parakompsas to nomisma tes eugeneias)* will be dragged down and carried into Tartarus itself and profound darkness. (*Praem.* 152)

What in the first passage is translated as "enjoyment of another's beauty" *(eumorphias)* may refer to marriage to a Gentile, though this is not clear. By following their natural appetites, eating forbidden food and consorting with (maybe marrying) forbidden people, the rebels/apostates have sold their freedom and threatened their eternal well-being. When in the second passage Philo alludes to Jews who are like the well-born man who "has debased the coinage of his noble birth," he may also allude to intermarriage as well as to a more general abandonment of Jewish laws. While there is an element of stereotyping

---

15. Translations of Philo are from the Loeb Classical Library edition unless otherwise indicated.

in *Virt.* 182—the lists are common enough, the proselytes represent all virtue and the apostates all vice—the most significant element is that they are seen as a contrasting pair. For while some think that the "rebels from the holy laws" refers to those who disobey rather than defect, the more natural sense is that if those in one group are those who enter the community, those in the other are those who leave it. Similarly, in the second passage, the contrasting fates of the virtuous proselytes, who will be especially prized in heaven, and those who abandon their privileged inheritance, who will get carried into "Tartarus itself and profound darkness," suggest an allusion to two opposites—those who join and those who abandon a community. In each case, the allusion to intermarriage is oblique, but Wolfson has made a case for this interpretation, as he has for distinguishing the Jews alluded to here from the "Yom Kippur" Jews (*Spec.* 1.186) who sat lightly on religious observance but once a year, or from those who were lured by the attractions of the Gentile world but made no deliberate break with their community.[16] The language Philo uses to describe these "apostate" Jews, the dire fate he envisages for them, and the contrast between them and

---

16. Wolfson (1947.1:73–77); originally followed by Feldman (1960:227), but not recently (1993:79–82). It is the context rather than the terms themselves that might support Wolfson. *Eumorphia* literally means "beauty of form" (cf. Josephus, *Ant.* 10.186; 15.23), and can be used of men (Philo, *Opif.* 136; *Ios.* 40, 268), animals (*Leg.* 2.75), slaves (*Spec.* 2.34; *Flacc.* 149), and idols (*Spec.* 1.29), as well as women (*Post.* 117; *Sobr.* 12; *Abr.* 93). It probably refers to beautiful women in *Spec.* 4.82, one of those things (like money and power) that uncontrolled appetites desire. *Testament of Judah* 14:3 conveys the sense of promiscuous sex. Thus desire for beautiful women rather than marriage to foreign women is all that the terminology suggests. Elsewhere Philo specifically mentions the dangers of intermarriage, especially as it affects offspring (*Spec.* 3:29; cf. *Jub.* 30:11). When recalling biblical instances of intermarriage, Philo takes a benign view and minimizes the foreign element in the relationships. Is this because it was not a pressing issue for him (Feldman 1993:77–79) or because it was sufficiently significant that the wise course was to take a gentle line and hope for the conversion of the pagan partner (Mendelson 1988:73–74)? The food laws are seen by Philo as a form of moral discipline (*Spec. Leg.* 4.100ff.). In a number of writings (e.g., 4 Macc 5:6ff.), adherence to the food laws epitomizes faithfulness to Judaism. "Debasing the coinage" is a common metaphor in Philo and alludes to the transgression of various personal or civic ideals (*Conf.* 159; *Fug.* 171, 208; *Spec.* 3.38, 176; 4.47; *Contempl.* 41). A reference to intermarriage in *Praem.* 152 is at most a possibility.

faithful proselytes suggest that they were of a different order from the casually unobservant.[17]

That intermarriage, and the resulting malign influence of "foreign" women, was seen as a problem is clear from other passages in Philo. In the recasting of the story of the Midianite women, it is central to the story (*Spec.* 1.54–58). In another allusion to it, the foreign women rouse the Israelites to a pitch of longing and lust and then announce: "You must not be permitted to enjoy my favors until you have left the ways of your fathers and become a convert to honoring what I honor. That your conversation is sincere will be clearly proved to me if you are willing to take part in the libations and sacrifices which we offer to idols of stone and wood and other images" (*Mos.* 1.295–305; cf. *Virt.* 34–44). The story is from the past, but the issue it addresses may well have continued into the present.

In describing the virtues of the young Moses, Philo contrasts him with those whom wealth has corrupted: they have an inflated view of themselves, despise the poor, abandon the ancestral laws, adopt other modes of life, forget the past, and satisfy themselves with the present (*Mos.* 1.30–31). These Jews, succumbing to the "vulgar delusion of social ambition," discard anything that stands in the way of their advancement in the Gentile world. Wolfson colorfully describes the imaginary progress of socially ambitious Alexandrian Jews "from the front row of the synagogue to a place at the tail end of the mystery processions of the heathen."[18]

Then there were those Jews exposed through education and social and civic life to the ideals and conventions of the pagan world. Philo himself was one such, and he gives a rich sense of the exposure to pagan culture and religion that came from the schools, theaters, sports, clubs, and guilds of Alexandria, most of which it appears he experienced.[19]

17. Feldman (1993:80) denies a reference to intermarriage and thinks that Philo is speaking not of apostates but of those who do not keep the commandments—part of his overall tendency to minimize the incidence of apostasy. He refers, unconvincingly, to the concern for repentance in *De virtutibus* and the rabbinic view that apostates remain in some sense Jews.

18. Quotations from Wolfson (1947.1:77). Feldman calls these unobservant rather than apostate Jews (1993:81).

19. Sandelin (1991:123–31); Borgen (1995:41–46).

For example, *Ebr.* 14–15, 20–23 appear to attack those who joined clubs or guilds for the wrong reasons and got drawn into morally destructive behavior (which some Jews therefore presumably did), yet *Ebr.* 20 seems to imply that the prudent can join and benefit. Philo seems ambivalent and does not spell out the distinction, except perhaps to imply that only the wise and self-controlled, like himself, for example, could participate without danger. Yet Philo clung tenaciously to his Jewish roots, condemned those who did not do the same, and promoted the earlier Alexandrian view (Aristobolus, Eupolomus, Artapanus) that all that was good in Greek philosophy had been borrowed from Judaism. No doubt others, like Philo's nephew, drifted away, perhaps without actively turning against their cultural and religious heritage (even if, in his military capacity, Alexander Tiberius gave short shrift to Jewish troublemakers).

But for some, exposure to Hellenism led to disenchantment with Judaism. Some queried and ridiculed the literal meaning of the law (*Agr.* 157; *QG* 1.53; 4.168; *Conf.* 4.9–10) or abandoned literal observance in favor of allegorical understanding (*Migr.* 86–93). Philo urges on the literalists consideration of the deeper (often allegorical) meaning of the law, while insisting that this does not require abandoning literal understanding or observance. The two are neatly distinguished but held together in *Conf.* 14 and 190. The identity of the groups that Philo tries to enlighten remains unclear, but it appears that they, like Philo, were interpreters of their tradition, not defectors from it. Others, however, went further, and derided and denounced the law:

> Persons who cherish a dislike of the institutions of our fathers and make it their constant study to denounce and decry the Laws find in these and similar passages openings as it were for their godlessness. "Can you still," say these impious scoffers, "speak gravely of the ordinances as containing the canons of truth? For see your so-called holy books contain also myths, which you regularly deride when you hear them related by others. And indeed," they continue, "it is needless to collect the numerous examples scattered about the Law-book, as we might had we leisure to spend in exposing its failings. We have but to remind you of the instances which lie at our very feet and ready to hand." (*Conf.* 2)

This is a more serious matter—not querying the interpretation or application of the law, but deriding and rejecting it: the law is no different from any other myth and contains no more truth. Who were these "impious scoffers"? They might have been non-Jews, Alexandrian intellectuals who knew enough about Jewish traditions to expose and challenge them. Sometimes this is part and parcel of a view that they cannot be Jewish because Judaism did not have defectors—a circular and unhelpful form of reasoning. But usually they are taken to be Jews, sometimes Jews inclined toward "gnostic" speculation, whose understanding of the Torah has moved beyond variant interpretation to outright rejection.[20] These may have been the sort of impious philosophers whom Philo calls the "sons of Cain" (*Post.* 35–40) and elsewhere accuses of atheism (*Mut.* 61), those who believe the human mind is the measure of all things, including sacred tradition. Or perhaps they were those described as follows:

> I have now described without any reservation the curses and penalties which they will deservedly suffer who disregard the holy laws of justice and piety, who have been seduced by the polytheistic creeds (*polytheios doxais*) which finally lead to atheism (*atheotes*), and have forgotten the teaching of their nation and their fathers, in which they were trained from their earliest years to acknowledge the One in substance, the supreme God, to whom alone all must belong who follow the truth unfeigned instead of mythical figments. (*Praem.* 162)

Such uprooted Jewish intellectuals thus effectively abandoned their own heritage, pushing up against, and in some cases beyond, the limits of their community.[21]

That apostasy could take a more serious turn is indicated by Philo's treatment of the Midianite incident in Numbers 25. Compared with Josephus (above), he places considerably more emphasis on the actions

---

20. Introducing the term "gnostic" raises a host of historical and chronological issues that are best left to one side in this context. Suffice it to say that later and better-documented forms of Gnosticism are often thought to have their roots in the earlier speculations of disenchanted Jews.
21. Wolfson (1947.1:78–85).

of the avenger, Phinehas, against those who "surrender treacherously the honor due to the One" *(kathyphientai ten tou henos timen)* or "desert the ranks of piety and religion" *(lipontes ten . . . eusebeian kai hosiotetos taxin)*. These should suffer the utmost penalties from the people who may act as "councillors, jury, governors, accusers, witnesses, laws, people," just as Phinehas did of old *(Spec. 1.54–57)*. Torrey Seland has suggested that Philo is not only alluding to a contemporary problem with apostates, but also legitimizing severe vigilante action against them.[22] That is, what we read here is not merely a piece of exegetical fancy but a response to a real issue in his community. This view is strengthened by other passages in Philo where contemporary echoes are unmistakable:

> Further if anyone cloaking himself under the name and guise of a prophet and claiming to be possessed by inspiration leads us on to the worship of the gods recognized in the different cities, we ought not to listen to him and be deceived by the name of prophet. And if a brother or son or daughter or wife or a housemate or a friend however true, or anyone else who seems to be kindly disposed, urge us to a like course, bidding us fraternize with the multitude, resort to their temples, and join in their libations or sacrifices, we must punish him as a public and general enemy, taking little thought for the ties that bind us to him; and we must send round a report of his proposals to all the lovers of piety, who will rush with a speed which brooks no delay to take vengeance on the unholy man and deem it a religious duty to seek his death. *(Spec. 1.316)*

Several interesting points emerge here: first, that defection could mean not only abandoning Jewish practice but also embracing pagan worship; second, that one could be seduced into such behavior by charismatic prophets—perhaps not so surprising—but equally tellingly by family and friends; and third, that Philo encouraged a severe and violent reaction: speedy reprisal, public denunciation, and

22. Seland (1995:103–14). He argues (1995:1–41) that Philo approved of lynching for egregious misdeeds: idolatry, false prophecy, perjury, and sorcery *(Spec.* 1.54–57; 1.315–18; 2.252–54; and 3.96–97 respectively).

death. Unless he is speaking of proselytes, of which there is no indication, the relatives and friends as well as the false prophets were presumably Jews. What did the defectors, the prophets, and the families think they were doing? Were they merely trying to accommodate to the religious preferences of their friends and neighbors, or to participate like other citizens in the civic cults? Could they have imagined that they were not compromising their commitment to Judaism but merely adjusting and refining it? Were they perhaps returning the favor of pagan sympathizers who shared in aspects of synagogue life without giving up all ties to their own cults? These are all fascinating questions to which we have no answers. We have the uncompromising view of Philo, and it is hard not to think that most Jews would have shared his view that participation in pagan cults was tantamount to abandoning a fundamental, biblically endorsed, defining element of their own tradition.

Philo's identification of at least five reasons for defection—the consumption of forbidden foods, intermarriage (or forbidden sexual relations), the lure of wealth and social ambition, intellectual disaffection, and the seductive pull of charismatic leaders, relatives, and friends—is particularly interesting. Unlike many of our other examples, they are not presented as a response to oppression or an immediate crisis. They are more varied, reflect a more routine response to the everyday experience of Jews in the diaspora, and suggest that we should think more in terms of a penumbra than of a sharply defined boundary between Jews and the outside world. They also bring us closer to some of the motives for apostasy identified in studies of the modern world. Thus, although we are dependent on Philo's viewpoint, and not all of those he defined as apostates may have seen themselves that way, much of what he says has the ring of truth. Striking, too, is Philo's blunt response to apostasy, encouraging his fellow Jews to exact the most extreme of penalties—though apart from the massacre of the three hundred apostates (3 Macc 7:15), which belongs to another setting, we have no evidence that Philo was taken at his word. Of course, largely because of Philo, we know a great deal more about the Jews in Alexandria than about those in other diaspora communities. It would not be unreasonable to suppose, however, that in other communities there were Jews who went through similar experiences. As to their numbers we cannot say, but, even if few, they remain a significant minority.[23]

Further insight into Jewish defections can be gleaned from the report that, during the reign of the emperor Domitian (81–96 CE), there was an attempt to crack down on those who had avoided paying the Jewish tax, among whom were Jews who tried to cover up their Jewish origins:

> The treasury department took its harshest measures against the Jews in particular. Those accused before it were not professed Jews but followed the Jewish way of life, and those who concealed their origin and had not paid the tribute imposed on the nation. (Suetonius, *Dom.* 12.2; trans. Whittaker 1984)

The Jewish tax was imposed by the Romans at the end of the Jewish War, replacing the old temple tax that Jews had been allowed to collect prior to that. Now the range of Jews liable for the tax was extended and the money directed to Roman coffers, creating a financial penalty, but also a symbol of ignominious defeat. Whether these Jews had made a decisive break with their community, drifted away from observance of Jewish customs (and thus considered themselves not really Jewish any longer), or kept their origins a secret to avoid the taxman is not clear, but either one of the first two seems more likely in view of the publicly observable nature of much Jewish practice. And if it seems unlikely that the tax alone, which most Jews managed to pay, would have precipitated sudden defection, then the most likely group in mind are Jews who had already in practice severed their ties with the Jewish community and now no longer wished to be counted as Jews. Rigorous collection of the tax merely brought things to a head, forcing them to declare

---

23. Feldman (1960:228–29), in contrast to Wolfson (1947.1:83) and Baron (1952.2:233), thinks they were few, an opinion he later repeats (Feldman 1986:105; 1993:79–83). He points to the anti-Semitism rife in Alexandria and the fact that only three apostates are known by name. In fact, we know a few more than three (though Helicon [*Legat.* 166–70], mentioned by Feldman, was not certainly a Jew—as he now notes in 1993:81–82), but this tells us little, since traditions do not usually celebrate defectors. Anti-Semitism may also have been as much a reason for leaving as for staying in the Jewish community.

their allegiance—though in this case it did them no good.[24] Martin Goodman has noted that these Jewish defectors were probably a significant group, judging by Suetonius's fairly sympathetic portrayal of them compared to his usually dismissive attitude toward Judaism and by the prominence accorded Nerva's removal of *calumnia* from the *fiscus Judaica* when he succeeded Domitian (Goodman 1989:40–44; 1994b:332).

As we saw above, rabbinic traditions use a variety of overlapping terms for apostates that do not always leave us with a clear idea of the finer distinctions between apostates and heretics or different sorts of apostates. Usually, too, their discussions identify issues but not individuals. One individual, however, stands out—the notorious apostate in early rabbinic traditions, Elisha ben Abuyah, often called *Aḥer* ("the other"). A prominent rabbi, he came to epitomize apostasy from Judaism in rabbinic tradition. An extended account is given in the Jerusalem Talmud, *Ḥag.* 2:1:

> Four entered the Garden [or Paradise]. One cast a look and died. One cast a look and was stricken [or went mad]. One cast a look and cut among the shoots. One entered safely and departed safely.
>
> Ben Azzai cast a look and died. . . .
>
> Ben Zoma cast a look and was stricken. . . .
>
> Aḥer cast a look and cut among the shoots.
>
> Who is Aḥer? Elisha ben Abuyah, who slew the young scholars of the Torah.
>
> They say: He used to kill every disciple he saw mastering the Torah. Moreover, he used to enter the schoolhouse, and when he saw the students in the presence of the teacher he would say, "What are

---

24. In her later role as Titus's mistress, Berenice might have been considered an apostate, but she is not so accused. Certainly earlier in her career she insisted a potential husband first be circumcised, and also undertook Nazirite vows (Josephus, *War* 2.14–15). Like Berenice, Josephus supported the Flavians. But although his opportunism during the war caused indignation and resentment (*War* 3.432–42), and much of his appendix to the *Antiquities* (*Life*) is an attempt to answer the charge that he was a coward and traitor, Josephus was not an apostate. His commitment to Judaism, as is clear from *Against Apion*, remained, despite what others thought of his political judgment.

these doing here? This one should be a mason; this one should be a carpenter; this one should be a fisherman; this one should be a tailor."

Elisha said, "Once I was passing before the Holy of Holies riding upon my horse on the Day of Atonement which happened to fall upon a Sabbath, and I heard an echo coming out of the Holy of Holies saying, 'Repent, children, except for Elisha ben Abuyah, for he knew my power yet rebelled against me!'"

Some say [he defected] because he saw the tongue of Rabbi Judah the Baker, dripping blood, in the mouth of a dog. He said, "This is the Torah, and its reward! This is the tongue that was bringing forth words of the Torah as befits them. This is the tongue that labored in the Torah all its days. This is the Torah, and this is its reward. It seems as though there is no reward [for righteousness] and no resurrection of the dead."

But some say that when his mother was pregnant with him, she passed by some heathen temples and smelled their particular kind of incense. And the odor pierced her body like the poison of a snake.[25]

It is difficult to know what historical nuggets there may be in the many legends associated with Elisha, but it is worth reviewing the more prominent explanations of his defection in later tradition.[26] The beginning of the excerpt above gives an epitome of the famous rabbinic legend about the visit to paradise of four leading rabbis and the fate that befell them. It is not quite clear what "cut among the shoots" means, but in context it seems to refer to his active role in discouraging study and observance of the Torah, as in the section that follows. A later version, which identifies the famous Rabbi Akiba as the only one who survives the mystical journey unscathed, indicates that Elisha's downfall was that he saw the seated Metraton and drew the conclusion that there were two powers in heaven (b. Ḥag. 14b–15a; cf t. Ḥag. 2:3). Both Alan Segal (1977) and Christopher Rowland (1982) argue that the story of the ascent into paradise, like many other traditions about Elisha, shows

25. Excerpts from the translation by and using the text division of Jacob Neusner.
26. The standard encyclopedia articles are useful, but they were superseded by Segal (1977:60–67); Stroumsa (1981); Rowland (1982:309–14); and Ayali (1988–89). See also Assaraf (1991); and, above all, Goshen-Gottstein (2000).

considerable evidence of legendary accretion, as is to be expected of an arch-heretic (like Simon Magus in Christianity). But they agree that the core of the story, Elisha's heretical speculation about God and his heavenly attendants, is not out of place in second-century Judaism.

In what is by far the most thorough and subtle discussion of ben Abuyah, however, Alon Goshen-Gottstein (2000) diverges from almost all previous studies, which find a historical core in the rabbinic reports. He denies the historicity of all rabbinic statements about him, except those early traditions that record his teachings neutrally, without any suggestion that he was an apostate or in any way suspect.[27] For example, he was not Rabbi Meir's teacher, did not indulge in gnostic speculation, did not defy the law or encourage other Jews to do so, and, above all, did not apostatize. His apostasy is nothing more than a rabbinic fiction, the stories about which serve the hermeneutical and theological interests of the tellers and bear no relationship to historical reality. The root of the problem lay in the early, but stylized, version of the paradise visit found in *t. Ḥag.* 2:3–4, in which ben Abuyah is cast as the epitome of the wicked sage (Akiba is the good sage and the other two somewhere in between). Once this initial move was made, all the other traditions that supposedly describe how he expressed his defection (e.g., riding his horse on the Sabbath), or that try to explain how such a famous sage could end up this way (e.g., he was contaminated by paganism while still in the womb), are attempts to deal with the tradition initiated by the authors of *t. Ḥag.* 2:3–4.[28] Many of Goshen-Gottstein's arguments about the hermeneutical interests of the rabbis and the traditions they invented to express them are persuasive, and he points out the dangers of arbitrarily picking and choosing from the various traditions in order to get back to a historical core. In the end, however, his arguments do not provide a persuasive explanation of the negative traditions associated with ben Abuyah. Why, for example, was he chosen to be the epitome of the wicked sage? Was this purely an

---

27. These are *m. Abot* 4:20 and *b. Mo'ed Qaṭ.* 20a. He also uses *Abot de Rabbi Nathan* A 40 as an early source, though many would date it later.

28. Goshen-Gottstein (2000) puts the various accounts in the following sequence, the earlier in each case being the basis for the later despite their different agendas: *t. Ḥag.* 2:3–4; *y. Ḥag.* 77b; *b. Ḥag.* 15a–b; *y. Ḥag.* 77b–c.

arbitrary decision, or was it because his reputation was already fixed? Why did he get the nickname *Aher*? And, while some stories clearly look like legendary accretions to an earlier tradition, others are impressively varied and historically plausible.[29]

Most interesting, and historically rooted in an early period, are the allusions to profound disillusionment caused by the persecution following the Bar Kokhba rebellion, when righteous and faithful Jews were brutally slaughtered for holding to their tradition. This is implied in the gory fate of Judah the Baker, a righteous and learned rabbi who nevertheless was felled by Roman savagery. It would also explain the core tradition that ben Abuyah discouraged young students of the Torah on the grounds that it made no sense if their fate was to be like that of Judah. He is said to have openly revealed the irrevocable nature of his defection in other ways too—he desecrated the Sabbath by riding near the synagogue in Tiberias, for example.[30] This public gesture is perhaps reflected in a later report of Jewish defection, but this time by an Alexandrian Jew:

> Zeno, an Alexandrian born a Jew, renounced in public the nation of the Jews in the way usual among them, driving the white ass through their so-called synagogue on the day of rest. This Zeno was by nature a kindly and holy person, but was rather sluggish in dialectic and mathematics. However, he had always aimed at learning something and used to ask about what he did not know, yet he only knew next to nothing. For he was most slow to apprehend and very ready to throw away what he had learned with difficulty because of his forgetfulness. (M. Stern 1984:678 [no. 550])

29. I did not find persuasive his argument that the nickname *Aher* ("other") is just an orthographic change from the word *Ehad* ("one," as in "one gazed and was smitten" in the Tosefta version) that is used in the paradise tradition. Nor was I persuaded that R. Meir is associated with ben Abuyah originally because of the connection between *Aher* ("other") and *Aherim* ("others"), where the latter is a term used in referring to anonymous rabbinic traditions ("others say that . . .") but is identified in some later traditions as R. Meir, in the sense that the teaching of "others" is to be taken as the teaching of R. Meir.

30. Anachronistically set on the Day of Atonement and near the sacred center of the Jerusalem Temple in the source quoted above.

Zeno, this source somewhat caustically says, was forgetful and slow-witted, though whether that was what caused his defection is not clear.

Elisha ben Abuyah's problems were far more profound, and they led him to doubt the justice of God and his control of events. That this may have been the root cause of his apostasy is both intriguing and plausible. The failure of the Bar Kokhba rebellion, the subsequent repression of Judaism and the death of many prominent Jews raised the problem of theodicy in the sharpest possible fashion and would have been enough to test the strongest of faiths.[31] It would have been neither the first nor the last time that historical events raised severe doubts about the justice, omnipotence, and love of God. It is also possible that this traumatic experience was mixed up in some way (a cause of?) with speculation about the divine being, perhaps along the lines of those who declared that there were two powers in heaven. It may be that Elisha moved in the direction of Gnosticism, and Gnostics (along with Christian Jews, Hellenized Jews and others) are probably to be included in the rabbinic definition of *minim* and those who believed in two powers. The possible connection between disillusionment following the Bar Kokhba rebellion and the turn to gnostic dualism presents intriguing possibilities for the origins of Jewish Gnosticism, at least of the second-century type. It has even been suggested that Elisha's nickname, *Aḥer*, might be the equivalent of the Greek *allogenes* and might link him with those Sethian Gnostics who saw themselves as descendants of "another seed," a third and distinctive race of strangers (Stroumsa 1981). However that may be, it is entirely plausible that the two things associated with Elisha were in some way connected, and, if so, we have two further causes of apostasy: doubts arising from events associated with a historical crisis; and, perhaps in response to the former, the search for an alternative intellectual system to explain the state of the world.

31. The length and severity of the persecution following the Bar Kokhba rebellion are disputed. The evidence is mainly rabbinic and late. See especially the discussion of Schäfer (1981:194–235). It is perhaps of some interest that Tertullian suggests that Marcion was driven by an obsession with the problem of theodicy. He was a contemporary of Aḥer and went in somewhat the same direction.

Finally, we need to consider two more ambivalent pieces of evidence that may add to our toll and cast further light on the phenomenon we are studying. First, the Dead Sea Scrolls produced by the Qumran community contain many attacks on those who were considered renegades. The "seekers after smooth things" (1QH 2:31–32; 4QpNah 1:2, 4), "men of power" (1QpHab 8:11–12), and the "wicked priest" (1QpHab 1:13; 8:8–13) all seem to refer to other Jews who were considered beyond the pale. But these are not apostates in the sense we are using the term, since they had never had any allegiance to the Qumran community in the first place. The perspective is sectarian, and the particular groups mentioned are merely the most egregious offenders among all those Jews who were not members of the community. All such Jews, and Gentiles too, were cursed and excoriated without restraint (1QS 1:18–2:18; 1QM 13:1–6). We do read of expulsion as an extreme penalty for those who defy the community and stubbornly follow their own path (1QS 2:16–23) and this may refer (at least hypothetically) to apostates of a sort, though in much the same way that some early Christians were viewed by their Christian opponents.[32] More interesting is the allusion in the Temple Scroll to Jewish defectors:

> If a man informs against his people, and delivers his people up to a foreign nation, and does harm to his people, you shall hang him on the tree, and he shall die. . . . And if a man has committed a crime punishable by death, and has defected into the midst of the nations and has cursed his people and the children of Israel, you shall hang him also on the tree, and he shall die. (11QT 64:6b–13a, trans. Yadin 1977–83.2:290)

This rewriting of Deut 21:22-23 that, by reversing the verbs "hang" and "die," justifies crucifixion as a form of death penalty seems to mention two related crimes: informers who place the Jews in danger; and defectors who, having committed a capital offense, flee to the Gentiles and curse their own people. The allusions and the date are uncertain. Yigael Yadin places it about 134 BCE, and sees it as an allusion to defectors from the Qumran community. Michael Wise has argued, however,

---

32. Lübbe (1986) thinks this may have been the original purpose of 4QTest.

that the Temple Scroll was not originally a sectarian document and may come from an earlier phase of Maccabean rule.[33] If so, it may reflect the crisis that precipitated the Maccabean rebellion and the way in which Jews who succumbed to Seleucid pressure were subsequently sometimes dealt with.

Last, we turn to a Jewish Christian, Paul, one of the best documented and most controversial examples of individuals who might be included in our list. Zealous Jews accused Paul of teaching Christian Jews to "abandon *(apostasian)* the teachings of Moses" (Acts 21:21), and the Ebionites saw him as an apostate from Judaism (Eusebius, *Hist. eccl.* 3.27.4). If we suppose that Acts and Eusebius are accurate, was there any basis for the two charges? There is little to support the view that Paul encouraged other Jews to neglect the Torah, and there are certainly those who vigorously defend him against the charge of apostasy. Dunn, for example, argues that "Paul could never have accepted that his apostleship to the Gentiles constituted apostasy from Israel. Quite the contrary, he was apostle to the Gentiles precisely as apostle *for* Israel, apostle *of* Israel" (Dunn 1998:269). The gist of his case is that Paul sees God's new dealings with the Gentiles through Christ to be a fulfillment or extension of his covenant with Israel and not its abrogation. Perhaps so, but this is to ignore the novelty of Paul's tendentious arguments about Abraham and Moses in Galatians 3–4 and his reflections on the fate of Israel in Romans 9–11 (eccentric enough in Christian, not to mention Jewish, circles) and the degree to which we can accept his own self-assessment. Would any non-Christian Jew have been convinced? And how important is Paul's own view of himself? Dunn (1998:270–71) is aware that such questions have to be asked, and he raises the question whether Paul was unrealistic or self-deceiving, whether he was de facto an apostate. But while admitting that Paul's attempt to redefine Israel did not persuade non-Christian Jews (and still has not), he prefers to call him a failure rather than an apostate.

Many others argue, however, that Paul is properly described as an apostate. Segal agrees, as the very title of his book indicates—*Paul the*

---

33. Yadin (1977–83.1:373–77). Wise argues for a date ca. 150 BCE and a nonsectarian origin (1990:121–27). He is reluctant to associate it with specific historical events, but the date he suggests would fit well with the aftermath of the Maccabean rebellion.

Convert: The Apostolate and Apostasy of Saul the Pharisee. He is particularly emphatic that whatever it was that Paul thought he was doing, he would have been judged by other Jews and Jewish Christians to be a renegade (Segal 1990:223, 290). Lloyd Gaston argues that Paul's identification with his Gentile converts and their gospel of salvation through Christ necessarily made him an apostate, despite seeing himself as one of the few faithful Israelites (Rom 11:1) and the probability that he continued to keep the commandments. His apostasy had to do with his apostolate.[34]

One of Barclay's premises is that apostasy is defined by societal reaction to an individual and not by that individual's self-assessment, and he suggests that for Jews the degree of assimilation (expressed by abandoning Jewish customs) would have been the key indicator of apostasy. His assessment of Paul is as follows: that it is a mistake to take too much notice of what Paul claims about himself (2 Cor 11:22; Rom 11:1), since his self-assessment is at any rate ambiguous (Phil 3:2-11); that we should not be overly impressed by the traditional and scriptural content of his thought; that he was strongly opposed by Jews (2 Cor 11:24) and other Jewish Christians (Gal 2:11-17) but continued obstinately to identify with the Jews (Romans 9–11) and thus exacerbated the reaction against him; that Paul's attempt to redefine Judaism from within did not find social expression (his churches were sociologically distinct from Judaism) nor did it persuade most of his fellow Jews. Thus "inasmuch as Paul was consistently repudiated as an 'apostate' by his contemporaries, the label fits historical reality."[35]

Gaston would go further and argue that Paul was consciously an apostate, in the sense that he propounded and identified himself with the covenant for the Gentiles in Christ.[36] This view of Paul seems essentially correct. The message he conveyed hit at the very heart of

34. Gaston (1987:76–79). In Gaston's view Paul also maintains the validity of the original covenant with Israel, i.e., Paul believed there were two covenants, one for Jews and another for Gentiles.

35. Barclay (1995b:119). Barclay (1996:381–95) takes up the issue at length. I shall return to the more theoretical side of his papers below.

36. Gaston (1987:79) qualifies this: "If Paul was occasionally in his own mind an apostate in the technical sense, much more important for his own self-consciousness was the sense of being one of the few faithful Israelites (Rom 11:1)."

Judaism as understood by his Jewish contemporaries, and, I suspect, he abandoned some Jewish practices when living among Gentiles (1 Cor 9:22; Gal 1:13-14; et al.). Paul is of exceptional interest: we know more about him than most; he was a reluctant apostate who remained ambivalent about his loyalties; he rejected Judaism not because he was disillusioned with it, but because he was possessed by another vision; and he is a classic example of one group's apostate becoming another group's convert.

Epigraphic Evidence

Our literary sources give us every reason to think that some Jews defected from their community, sometimes gradually and unobtrusively, sometimes suddenly in the face of a crisis, and sometimes violently. So the phenomenon existed. It is now useful to turn to an often more ambiguous source, but one that can further broaden the scope of our enquiry: epigraphic evidence.[37]

The relative value of, and the relationship between, literary and epigraphic sources have been much discussed. The former, it might be suggested, provide the broad picture into which the minutiae of the latter can be woven, while the latter provide the local detail essential for filling out and correcting the former. Sometimes these have been presented as competitive claims, but their relationship is more productively seen as complementary. Epigraphic evidence has much to offer: it deals with the nitty-gritty of life and reflects the concerns of all levels of society; it expresses views unfiltered by normative tradition; and it can usually be assigned a place and, with less certainty, a date. It is not necessarily unbiased—epitaphs and panegyrics on behalf of patrons and leaders have their own, often transparent, agendas—

---

37. The only attempt to collect epigraphic material relating to defectors known to me is Figueras (1990), in a section entitled "Jewish Syncretism and Defection to Paganism and Christianity." Borgen has a brief analysis of three inscriptions (1995:36–37). Barclay discusses most of the evidence at various points in his astute survey of diaspora Judaism (1996). Otherwise individual inscriptions are discussed in passing by editors of inscriptional collections or those interested in broader aspects of Jewish life.

and it is usually written with an audience in mind, but it does offer a slice of life that we otherwise do not see.[38]

Literary and historical texts, on the other hand, provide a linguistic context in which particular statements can be interpreted and, for all their biases, paint the bigger picture without which much of the surviving epigraphic evidence, where it made sense at all, would leave us with a seriously limited view of ancient life. It has been noted, for example, that epigraphic and archeological evidence alone would leave us with almost no sense of the practices and beliefs that were central in the lives of Jews in antiquity (Goodman 1994a:219). Epigraphic remains deal with limited areas of Jewish life and experience. Most common, for example, are epitaphs, followed by formal dedications and contracts. Only a few survive, and many of these are fragmentary and hard to read. They are usually laconic and sometimes use linguistic conventions peculiar to their genre. Relative to the overall population of Jews, their numbers are infinitesimally small, a recent estimate suggesting that Jewish epitaphs represent well below 0.001% of the total Jewish population in the Roman period (van der Horst 1991:79–80). Their geographic distribution, too, is uneven, since the bulk of our evidence comes from Africa (including Egypt) and Rome. All this, of course, is in addition to the vexed question of deciding which inscriptions are Jewish and which are not.[39]

1. Perhaps a good place to start is with the best-known and most ambiguous inscriptions relating to defectors:

> *hoi pote Ioudaioi my[riada] a'*
> the former *Ioudaioi* [gave] 10,000. (*CII* II:742)

Located in Smyrna and dating from the emperor Hadrian's rule (117–38 CE), it is part of a list of donors to the city. The *Ioudaioi* gave

---

38. For a general discussion of the nature of epigraphic evidence, see Trebilco (1991:2–3) and Millar (1983); the latter notes that some inscriptions are minor literary works in themselves, suggesting that the boundaries between epigraphic and literary sources should not be too clearly drawn.

39. On defining Jewish inscriptions, see Kraemer (1991); van der Horst (1991:16–18); Kant (1987:682–89); and van Henten and de Vaate (1996), who base their study on a critique of some of the material designated Jewish by Trebilco (1991).

a total of 10,000 drachmas, not a large donation, since some individuals gave 70,000, and ten other individuals gave a total of 10,000. This may suggest that the Jews were a group rather larger than ten (Smallwood 1976:507). It presents, in context, no transcriptional problems. The ambiguity lies in the peculiar use of *pote* and the fluid range of the word *Ioudaios*. The earliest editors (*CIG* 3148; *IGRR* iv.1431; *CII* II:742) took it to refer to "former Jews" who had renounced their Judaism and made their donation in order to gain civic rights and social acceptance. Thomas Kraabel proposed that it should be translated "'people formerly of Judea,' perhaps immigrants from Palestine, now doing their civic duty as residents of Smyrna" (1982:455). Presumably these could have been non-Jews (Kraabel does not specify), which would eliminate a reference not only to defectors but to Jews as well. Kraemer (1989:43), in turn, suggested that this interpretation could be extended to several other inscriptions from Asia Minor.

Kraabel's translation is inherently improbable and is offered with virtually no supporting evidence. Yet it has frequently been adopted,[40] in part, I suspect, from a vague sense that defection from Judaism was extremely rare and should be assumed only when the evidence unavoidably points that way.

The term *Ioudaios* (Latin *Iudaeus*) has indeed a range of possible meanings. It can be used as a name, a rare and early meaning. That it could be used to refer to pagan sympathizers rather than Jews or proselytes seems unlikely.[41] The geographic meaning "Judean" is found in earlier sources and perhaps in Josephus's phrase "by origin a Judean"

40. For example, Trebilco (1991:175) simply says that Kraabel has shown that the phrase means "former Judeans"! Solin (1983:646) says that if Kraabel is right, it is an extremely rare use of *Ioudaios*. Van der Horst (1991:69n24) thinks it not probable but unprovable. Harland (2003:202–3) has revived the argument and thinks that the description of one Aurelius as "formerly *(prin)* of Pieria" provides an analogy.

41. So van der Horst (1991:69–71) and Williams (1997a:250–53), arguing against Kraemer's view that it is often used as a name and that it could refer to pagan sympathizers too. Dio Cassius does say that non-Jews who lived according to Jewish laws were called Jews, but he may refer to proselytes rather than sympathizers (*Roman History* 37.17.1). There is no clear inscriptional evidence for sympathizers called *Ioudaioi*, and at any rate, it would be hard to distinguish them from Jews and proselytes.

(*Ioudaiaos to genos*).[42] Yet by the Roman period, the term refers over-whelmingly, perhaps exclusively, to Jews wherever they hailed from.[43] Common usage thus does not favor the translation "Judeans." Further, it has been noted, it would be highly unlikely—if *Iudaeus* regularly meant "Judean"—that so many of them would have Latin cognomen (Solin 1983:648; van der Horst 1991:70). If the reference is thought to be to non-Jewish Judeans, it would be surprising to find them advertising their links with a people who had recently been involved in a series of bloody revolts under Trajan and (depending on the inscription's date) perhaps under Hadrian too.[44] In addition, the normal way of expressing place of origin in inscriptions is by city rather than country of origin, using the preposition *apo* plus the city name or simply the city name in the genitive. If an ethnicon is used, it is usually in the nominative (Kant 1987:687n97, 707; Williams 1997b:252).[45] The evidence thus points strongly to the translation "the former Jews."

Are there any arguments that favor Kraabel's view? Solin, who views it at best as a rare exception to the general use of *Ioudaios*, suggested two parallels that, in the end, do not strengthen the case.[46] Some

---

42. Cohen notes, however, that Josephus's phrase is an "archaic usage" (1994:36–37).

43. See the lucid discussion in van der Horst (1991:69–70) and especially Williams (1997a:252–53), who has an acute discussion of the inscriptional use of *Ioudaios/Iudaeus* in general and the Smyrna inscription in particular. *Ioudaios* can convey the sense of an external perspective, Jews talking to or being talked about by non-Jews, as distinct from the term *Israel*, which expresses an inner-Jewish perspective (Tomson 1986), though this distinction does not apply uniformly to the evidence.

44. Williams (1997a:251–52). She notes too that if we could date the inscription more precisely (which we cannot) to the period after 135 CE when Judea was renamed Syria-Palestine, that would help settle the matter. It might be possible to argue that they were demonstrating their benevolence and reliability at precisely the time when Jews (under Trajan and Hadrian) had been involved in open revolt (Trebilco 1991:175). If they were Jews from Judea, they might have emigrated precisely to get away from the troubles in Judea.

45. Cohen makes the same point more briefly when he notes that non-Jews from Judea would be called simply "Judeans," not "former Judeans" (1990:221n5). Barclay also notes that there is no supporting evidence for the view that those from Judea would be described as "the former Judeans" (1996:333).

46. So Williams (1997a:252). She notes that the reading *Iuda(eus)* in *CIL* XIV:4624 has now been corrected to *Iuda*, and that the use of the abbreviation *v.s.f.* in *CII* II:643

think it would be odd to record one's apostasy in a barely noticeable phrase buried in a long list of donors (Kraabel 1982:455), while others have remarked—to the contrary—that it would be odd for "the former Jews" to advertise their apostasy in such a public way. Yet there are literary parallels to public defection (Antiochus in Josephus, *War* 7.47, and Elisha ben Abuyah, as we saw above), and it may be that the phrase was chosen by others as a convenient, collective way to describe this group of former Jews.[47] All in all, there seems nothing to be said for Kraabel's view, and we should take this inscription as clear evidence for Jewish defection.

2. We turn back several hundred years to what may be the earliest epigraphic reference to a Jewish defector:

> Moschos, son of Moschion, a Jew, as a result of a dream [has set up this stele] at the command of the god Amphiaraos and Hygeia, in accordance with the orders of Amphiaraos and Hygeia to write these things on a stele and set [it] up by the altar. (*CII* I²:711b, trans. Williams 1997b:258)

From the sanctuary of the healing god Amphiaraos in Oropus, between Attica and Boetia, and dated to the period 300–250 BCE, it records the manumission of the Jew Moschos, slave of Phrynidas. Moschos, the inscription continues, sought healing or help at the sanctuary. The gods Amphiaraos and Hygeia appeared to him in a dream and instructed him to erect the stele near the altar of the sanctuary. The implication is that Moschos followed the normal ritual process at Amphiorus, which involved incubation, sacrifice of a ram, and payment of a fee (Lewis 1957:264–65). Moschos declares that he is son of Moschion, a Jew, yet

---

does not indicate a pagan origin (and thus a geographic sense for *Iudaeus* in this inscription), since Jews did use *v.s.f.* (*votum solvit feliciter*—"willingly fulfilled his vow") and, at any rate, it could be an abbreviation for *vivus sibi fecit* ("erected for himself during his lifetime") as in Noy (1993.1:7).

47. Levinskaya thinks it was simply the name by which they were known in the city and that it may primarily have had an economic reference to Jews who once paid the *fiscus judaicus* but did so no longer, contributing instead to their city of residence (1996:210n11).

he engages in what were, from a Jewish perspective, decidedly impious practices (Williams 1997b:255). Is he thus declaring a change of allegiance or implying that his engagement in pagan religious rites was merely a temporary concession to deal with some sort of crisis? It seems to be a clear example of extreme syncretism or, better, of defection—though, as we shall see, the line between syncretism and defection is not always easy to draw.

3. A series of inscriptions at a temple of the god Pan raises similar issues:

> Bless God *(theos)*! Theodotos [son] of Dorion, a Jew, rescued from the sea. (*CII* II:1537 = Horbury and Noy 1992:121)

> Ptolemaios [son] of Dionysios, a Jew, blesses the god *(ton theon)*. (*CII* II:1538 = Horbury and Noy 1992:122)

> Two inscriptions by one Lazarus, who came "three times" *(triton)* or perhaps, "with two others." (Horbury and Noy 1992:123, 124)

These are part of ninety inscriptions found around a temple complex at el-Kanais, Egypt, most of which are dedicated to "Pan of the Successful Journey," and are dated 150–80 BCE. The first two celebrate either rescue from a shipwreck or, less dramatically, a safe voyage. Frey thought them the product of Jews who were at the least "unorthodox" (*CII* II:1537–38), since they thought that they could give thanks either to Yahweh in a temple of Pan or to Pan because he was some sort of universal deity (*to pan* = "the all").[48] Others have noted some unusual features: the celebrants acknowledge their Jewish parentage; they give thanks ambiguously to a "god," who could be either Pan or Yahweh, while most of the other inscriptions on the site specifically mention Pan; and the inscriptions are found on a rock face west of the temple, slightly away from the main sanctuary. Their distinctive language and location are thus, for some, evidence that Theodotos and Ptolemaios deliberately tried to avoid any semblance of apostatizing (Bernand 1972:105–9; Horbury and Noy 1992:207–8). The significance of their

---

48. Frey (*CII* II:445); similarly Figueras (1990:203).

location has perhaps been overplayed (Kant 1987:685n85), especially when we note that one of the Lazarus inscriptions, identified as Jewish by the name alone, is inside the main sanctuary (the restoration of the name in this inscription is uncertain: Horbury and Noy 1992:212). That Theodotos and Ptolemaios assert their Jewish identity may represent only their own assessment. Defectors, typically, do not declare themselves as such; indeed, they often protest the opposite. The term *theos* is ambiguous, but given the location in and around a sanctuary of Pan, it is not hard to imagine how most people would have understood it. Was Pan then more a concept than a deity, invoking whom was as innocuous as when we say (as perhaps ancient Jews did) "good luck" without necessarily conjuring up the deity of fortune?[49] Perhaps, but no evidence has been offered to support this, and the use of worn phrases like "good luck," or "Hades," or even invocations of ancestral gods (the *dis manibus* formula) are not the same as deliberately carving an inscription at a sanctuary dedicated to a figure widely regarded as the god of seafarers, among other things. Here the location speaks strongly against innocent ambiguity.[50] If these Jews honored a pagan deity, as seems most probable, they perhaps saw no conflict with their understanding of Judaism. Or it may indicate that they had abandoned their Jewish roots in favor of a more relaxed accommodation to pagan polytheism. Whatever they thought about their behavior, it placed them beyond what most Jews would have defined as acceptable limits.

4. The following comes from Asia Minor about 150 BCE:

Nicetas, a Jerusalemite from "Iasos" *(Iasonos)* donated ten drachmae. (*CII* II:749)

49. Goodenough (1956) thought the "good luck" *(agathe tyche)* inscriptions from the Bosporus were Jewish; others think they point to judaizing pagans (Kant 1987:684n81).

50. On the use of terms like "Hades," shorn of their mythological force, see van der Horst (1991:152); Lifshitz (1962:66–70); and Kant (1987:683). The recent consensus seems to be that Jews did use the *dis manibus* ("to the departed spirits") formula (Kraemer 1991:155–58; Kant 1987:683), but Rutgers argues that most such inscriptions are not Jewish, and if found in a Jewish context, they come from Jewish converts (1995:268–73)—a view not unlike Frey's (*CII* II:445). Off-the-shelf tombstones may have come with the formula already inscribed, and there is evidence for secondary use merely to block off a new tomb.

There is some ambiguity in the transcription—*Iasonos* may be the name Jason rather than the town Iasos in Asia Minor—but it does not affect my argument. The name appears on a list of donors to a Dionysus festival. Because he came from Jerusalem, Nicetas/Jason is identified as a Jew—a probable but not certain conclusion. If he was, his public association with the Dionysus festival was something most Jews would have avoided (Borgen 1995:36), especially if we assume "that after paying his contribution he enjoyed the feast which he helped finance" (Barclay 1996:322). Perhaps he saw it as part of his civic duty, causing no threat to his Jewish identity, or perhaps his sense of identity with Judaism had been significantly weakened.

5. From Gorgippia, Russia, about 41 CE:

> To the most high God, Almighty, blessed *(theoi hypsistoi pantokratori eulogeto)* in the reign of the king Mithridates . . . Pothos, the son of Strabo, dedicated to the prayer house *(proseuchei)* in accordance with the vow his house-bred slave-woman, whose name is Chrysa, on condition that she should be unharmed and unmolested by any of his heirs under Zeus, Ge, Helios. (*CII* I:690; also I²:690; trans. Levinskaya 1996:239–40, based on her own transcription)

This is a classic example of the problems in defining Jewish inscriptions. The majority have accepted it as Jewish, arguing that the terms *pantokrator, eulogetos,* and *proseuche* are clearly Jewish. In this instance, therefore, *hypsistos* refers to Yahweh too.[51] Horsley has claimed that all of these terms could be pagan, and the oddity of introducing three pagan deities into a Jewish inscription would thus be removed.[52] But then it has been noted that the invocation of pagan deities was normal in judicial proceedings, and that Jews in Elephantine used pagan oath formulae—indeed, they may have been a legal requirement (Schürer

---

51. Frey took it to be Jewish and was followed by his reviser (*CII* I²:690), Lifshitz (1975), Kant (1987:684n81), and Trebilco (1991:136).

52. Horsley (1981:27). He notes that ruling out the pagan use of these terms in principle means that we might be overlooking precisely the evidence that inscriptions like this one might provide—though substituting one circular argument for another does not get us far. Van Henten and de Vaate (1996:25) also argue that the terms are variously used by Jews, Christians, and pagans and that a firm ascription is impossible.

1973–87:3.1.37). Jews would, on this view, have treated a reference to pagan gods as a mere formality.

Some of the issues remain unresolved. It is interesting to note that in none of the other manumission inscriptions from the Bosporus produced by Levinskaya (1996:231–42) does the invocation of pagan gods appear. This might lead us to doubt whether its use was such a routine matter. Also, the parallels with Elephantine are from a much earlier period and a different location and may not be relevant (van Henten and de Vaate 1996:25). Nor is the presence of the term *proseuche* a sure sign of a Jewish context. It was widely used by Jews to describe their meeting place, but it may have been used by pagans too.[53] *Theos hypsistos* was used by both pagans and Jews, even occasionally by Christians (Mitchell 1993:50n293), and the other divine descriptors do not certainly belong solely to Judaism. If it is of Jewish provenance, what do we make of the pagan formula? Is it a clear case of deliberate syncretism (Figueras 1990:204) or nothing more than the casual use of a pagan formula? Other evidence from the Bosporus might suggest the former; yet on the "Jewish" reading of the inscription, the enthusiastic invocation of Yahweh could be said to counteract the closing formula and to suggest that we should probably speak of accommodation but not of apostasy, though the issue remains finely balanced.

6. An inscription from Cyrene, dated to 60–61 CE, provides a list of the city magistrates *(nomophylakes),* including among them one *Eleazer, son of Jason.*[54] The name Eleazer was common among Cyrenian Jews, and it is usually assumed that he was a Jew too. The inscription is in the form of a dedication by the city magistrates to a deity (the name is lost), and it opens with the names of the past and present priests of Apollo. Other dedications from Cyrene by the city magistrates honor Apollo, Homonoia, and Aphrodite; and we may assume that one of

---

53. Trebilco (1991:242n42) thinks that pagans occasionally used it; he is followed by van Henten and de Vaate (1996:25). Levinskaya (1996:213–25) argues that they did not, except in the instance we are discussing, which she attributes to Gentile sympathizers influenced by Jews.

54. Originally published in *Quaderni del archeologia della Libia* 4 (1961) 16 (no. 2). It is discussed by Applebaum (1979:186–90) and Barclay (1996:235) and noted by Borgen (1995:37) as a possible example of defection with the caveat that we cannot assume that Jews like Eleazer saw themselves as abandoning their tradition.

these probably appeared here. The duties of the magistrates "were connected with registration and recording, with finance and with supervision over the proper administration of the law." They were thus the senior civic authorities, in all likelihood made up largely of the local aristocracy (Applebaum 1979:189–90, quotation 189).

It has long been recognized that significant adjustments would have had to be made when Jews joined the ranks of civic officialdom, since many of their duties routinely involved cultic activities associated with the city gods. Maybe there were instances where pagans made adjustments or allowances, but in this case, it seems that Eleazer went along with the standard rites of a pagan administration. Did this involve some sort of apostasy? Not according to Applebaum, who thinks that Eleazer's decision not to adopt a Greek name—as did many Cyrenian Jews, including those active in their communities—signals his faithfulness to Judaism (Applebaum 1979:186). Changing a name (or not) is, however, hardly a significant indicator of commitment to Judaism, as Applebaum himself indicates.[55] Eleazer must have made significant adjustments during his time as a magistrate, but it is possible that he, like other Jews in the same position, considered them acceptable compromises that did not seriously undermine his continuing commitment to Judaism. Like Philo, he could have been conscious of the dangers but convinced that he could himself survive, thus not only benefiting the city with his skills but also advancing the reputation of the Jewish community as a whole. It is certainly a more ambiguous example than some of those considered above.

7. In an inscription from Acmonia in Asia Minor, dated about 80–90 CE, we read of two brothers:

> This building was erected by Julia Severa; P[ublius] Tyrronios Klados, the head for life of the synagogue *(ho dia biou archisynagogos),* and Lucius, son of Lucius, head of the synagogue *(archisynagogos),* and Publius Zotikos, archon *(archon),* restored it with their own funds and with money which had been deposited. . . . and the synagogue honored them with a gilded shield. . . . (*MAMA* 6.264 = *CII* II:766)

---

55. Barclay (1996:235n9) questions whether Cyrenian Jews ever changed their names to signal alienation from Judaism.

This inscription has been understood to contain a reference to a Jewish defector—Julia Severa, a leading member of a distinguished Acmonian family. That she was high priestess of the imperial cult at Acmonia is clear, but that she was once a Jew cannot be proven; rather, she was a Gentile sympathizer who patronized the synagogue (Trebilco 1991:59). More intriguing is the observation of Borgen (1995:37) that Tyrronios Klados and Tyrronios Rapan, who is associated with Julia Severa in other inscriptions (e.g., *MAMA* 6.265 = *CII* II:765) and coins as a priest of the imperial cult, might be brothers or at least closely related. Mitchell notes: "The synagogue had been endowed by Julia Severa, a gentile, just as any other temple might be; closely related persons associated with her held advertised positions, on the one hand in the synagogue, and on the other in the hierarchy of emperor worship" (1993.2:9).[56] Does this mean that the one converted to Judaism or that the other defected from it? For Borgen "it is obvious that the *archisynagogos* was a member of the Jewish community." But things are not so obvious. Some pagan associations called themselves a *synagogoi* and their leaders *archisynagogoi* (Kraemer 1991:145; Horsley 1987:113), so we might be dealing with a pagan rather than a Jewish association. If, as is usually assumed, the reference is to a Jewish synagogue, Tyrronius Klados may have been a convert to Judaism, or perhaps a pagan patron given the honorific title of *archisynagogos* (Rajak and Noy 1993). Further, Tyrronius Rapon may have been a client or freedman of Tyrronius Klados rather than his brother. But if Tyrronius Rapon was born a Jew, then he was probably a defector—not the most secure of evidence, admittedly, but interesting nevertheless.

8. Of uncertain date is another inscription:

To the Iunones *(Iunonibus)!* Annia L[ucii], a liberated Jew [*Iuda*].
(*CII* I:576)

---

56. See further Ramsay (1897:637–40, 650–51) and Shepherd (1979:170). Tyrronius Rapon's priestly role is surmised largely from his association with Julia Severa and is never clearly stated, even in MAMA 4.265. Ramsay, with some tenuous arguments, concluded that they were married and that they were both Jews. That Tyrronius Rapon was a Jew may, as we have argued, be surmised on other grounds.

Frey (*CII* I:576) thought that apart from the term *Iuda,* the rest of the inscription smacked of paganism because of the invocation of pagan spirits (*Iunones*). David Noy (1993–95.1:19) thinks it undoubtedly pagan too, but others are equally convinced that it is Jewish (Kant 1987:683n79) and that it merely invokes spirits of the dead to protect the woman and her family. Kraemer wonders why she would use the appellation *Iuda* if she had renounced Judaism. She thinks Annia could have been a Jew who made offerings to pagan spirits or a proselyte who believed the Iunones were connected to childbirth, in which case "her simultaneous attachment to Judaism and her dedication to the Iunones seem considerably less incongruous" (1989:42–43, quotation 43). Williams (1997b:250) makes the interesting observation that Annia may have been named *Iuda* as a slave, since it was common for Greeks and Romans to name slaves after their country of origin. But, if correct, this means that she was from Judea, not that she was Jewish.

Again, the question of what is or what is not Jewish arises. Levinskaya notes that if *Iuda* was not used by pagans or Christians, and if Jews did not make dedications to pagan spirits, we must choose between how *Iuda* was used and what Jews can be assumed to have done (1996:211). She inclines to the latter, and thinks we must stretch our view of what Jews in reality did. This seems most likely, but, like the earlier example of Moschos, it raises the question of the line between accommodation and defection and the degree to which accommodation can be stretched to include marginal Jewish groups or individuals.

9. From North Africa we have a number of examples dated to the early fourth century CE:

Mose(s) (plus chi-rho symbol)

Sabbatiolus (plus chi-rho symbol)

In memory (with chi-rho symbol) of the blessed Istablicus who is also called Donatus. Installed by his brother Peregrinus, who is also called Mosattes, once a Jew (*de Iudeis*). (Le Bohec 1981:nos.1,66,75)

The significance of these epitaphs is that they appear to be in memory of men who were once Jews but were now Christians. Their jewishness is indicated by their names in the first two cases, and by the declaration that they were *de Iudeis* in the third. Le Bohec, who originally collected them, thought the first and third examples were converts to Christianity from Judaism. The second he understood to be a pagan judaizer who had converted, though it could as easily refer to Jews (Figueras 1990:205), or even to Christian judaizers (Kant 1987:707).[57] The Christian element in each case is the appearance of the chi-rho symbol.

Le Bohec was, I suspect, on the right track, but his evidence is not without its problems. The identification of ethnicity by name alone is problematic (Rutgers 1997). Devda (1997) suggested that "Moses" was not used by Jews until the ninth century, while Williams puts forward some counterexamples from the fourth century onward (all of them involving uncertain restorations of the text) (1997a:274). In general the chi-rho symbol appears to indicate Christian affiliation.[58] On balance we are probably dealing with cases of Jewish defections to Christianity. The phrase *de Iudeis* in the third example, as Kant (1987:707) notes, reminds us of *hoi pote Ioudaioi* from Smyrna.

10. Our final example comes from Italy, dates to the fourth to fifth century CE, and is fairly uncomplicated:

> Here lies Peter, who is [also called] Papario, son of Olympus the Jew, and the only one of his family/people *(gens)* who has deserved to attain the grace of Christ. . . . (*CII* I²:643a = Noy 1993:I.8)

There is not any doubt that we have here an example of Jewish conversion to Christianity, a not uncommon occurrence in the period after the conversion of the emperor Constantine, when many voluntary and forced conversions of Jews took place.

What then can we conclude from the epigraphic examples available to us? Certainly, the literary evidence indicates that there is no a priori reason to dismiss or deflate the phenomenon of Jewish defection. We have strong evidence that it occurred and good reason therefore to

---

57. Le Bohec (1981:167) argues that a Christian would not likely use the name Moses in North Africa, where anti-Semitism was rife.

58. Kraemer (1991:151) notes that the chi-rho symbol may in one instance appear with a menorah but assumes that if so it indicates a Jewish-Christian origin.

expect to find it turning up in epigraphic sources. Of the inscriptional examples, I would rank four (nos. 1, 2, 9, 10) as fairly certain examples of defection and two (5, 6) as unlikely. The remaining four present us with complex issues—mostly heuristic rather than transcriptional. The significance of names and other terms, their physical location and social context, and the extent to which they indicate Jewish identity complicate our attempts to interpret them, and in most of these respects they are inherently more problematic than literary sources.

More significantly, they often present us with a choice between a verdict of accommodation and one of defection. This is an inherently difficult issue. Defining a defector, like defining a heretic, is as much, if not more, the decision of others than of those supposedly involved, and what individuals assert of themselves (e.g., that "I am a Jew") does not necessarily contain the verdict of their community. Some people, after all, protest too much. In this, ancient sources are no more reliable than modern interpreters. Trebilco also notes: "In different situations the possibilities of completely avoiding pagan worship, of gaining exemption from involvement, of trying to avoid the occasions when pagan worship occurred, of 'turning a blind eye,' or of accepting pagan worship and taking part all remain" (1991:181–82). True enough, and the common wisdom is that the boundaries of Judaism were broader and more flexible than the normative traditions indicate, though we may become so familiar with this notion that our concept of Jewish accommodationism recognizes no limits—perhaps often those limits that the majority of Jews would have drawn rather more sharply than we are currently inclined to do. I would suggest that the notion of acceptable Jewish accommodationism, or syncretism, or whatever else we may wish to call it, has been overplayed and would thus tend to tip the ambiguous four cautiously into the camp of defectors too.

3

CHRISTIAN APOSTATES

Whereas the phenomenon of defectors has been raised and, in a few recent studies, discussed with a considerable degree of sophistication with respect to Judaism, it has scarcely appeared in discussions of early Christianity. As noted above, apart from a few older and limited surveys, the interest has largely been in apostasy as a theological issue, especially in relation to the eternal destiny of the apostate.

Part of the reason for this may be that in the New Testament the evidence for apostasy or defection is slight. To some degree this is a reflection of the nature of the documents, many of which deal with conflicting opinions within nascent Christian communities that had little collective sense of what defined their movement as a whole. In the absence of accepted orthodoxies and established boundaries, defection was difficult to define. Thus a great deal of energy is expended on attacking opponents who, whatever the authors thought of them, probably saw themselves as equally legitimate representatives of the Christian movement. Paul, for example, accuses the Galatians of reverting to paganism:

> Formerly, when you did not know God, you were enslaved to beings
> that by nature are not gods. Now, however, that you have come to

know God, or rather to be known by God, how can you turn back again to the weak and beggarly elemental spirits? How can you want to be enslaved to them again? You are observing special days and months and years. (Gal 4:8-10)

What exactly Paul is alluding to is not clear, though the letter elsewhere indicates that the Gentile Galatians have been persuaded to take on certain Jewish observances, most probably those promoted by other Jewish Christians active in the area. This suggests an internecine struggle between Paul and other Jewish Christians with an alternative version of the Christian message. Despite Paul's somewhat hysterical response, there is no reason to suppose that these Jewish Christians or the Galatians would have accepted Paul's view that they were abandoning the true faith and reverting to paganism. Far from it, for they would have argued that theirs was the legitimate understanding of the gospel. Indeed, the tussle over authority and legitimacy runs throughout the letter from the opening words onward.

A somewhat similar accusation is made in 2 Peter:

For if, after they have escaped the defilements of the world through the knowledge of our Lord and Savior Jesus Christ, they are again entangled in them and overpowered, the last state has become worse for them than the first. For it would have been better for them never to have known the way of righteousness than, after knowing it, to turn back from the holy commandment that was passed on to them. (2:20-21)

The recipients are warned against these "false teachers" (2:1; 3:17), whose program, unfortunately, we can only surmise from the words of their opponents. Polemical distortion and the use of rhetorical conventions make recovery of their views an uncertain business, but they appear to have had doubts about the parousia (3:4) and perhaps also an unusual view of Jesus's first coming (1:16). They also perhaps understood Christian freedom to include a license for self-indulgence, pleasure and personal gain (2:2-3, 10, 13, 15-16, 18). Their views may have been based in part on a distinctive reading of Paul's letters (3:15-16), and there are good arguments for detecting the influence of early gnostic or Epicurean ideas. Even allowing for rhetorical distortion, it is not difficult to imagine a group that looked different from most other forms of Christianity current at the time, perhaps sufficiently different to qualify for the accusation of apostasy (which is effectively what 2:20-21 does). But the fact remains that they are still influential and still involved in the community, enough at least to provoke the pseudonymous author vigorously to attack them.

In a similar vein, the author of 1 Timothy writes about those who are disrupting the community in Ephesus:

> Now the Spirit expressly says that in later times some will renounce the faith *(apostesontai tines tes pisteos)* by paying attention to deceitful spirits and teachings of the demons, through the hypocrisy of liars whose consciences are seared with a hot iron. They forbid marriage and demand abstinence from foods, which God created to be received with thanksgiving by those who believe and know the truth. (4:1-3)

It is difficult to probe beneath this barrage of name-calling to discover what the dissident Christians stood for, but abstinence from marriage and foods seems specific enough for us to accept the attribution. 1 Timothy 5:23 also implies an interest in asceticism in the community. In several places, the author is scathing about their interest in speculation, myths and genealogies, old wives' tales and verbal sparring (1:4-7; 4:7; 6:4), all perhaps summed up in what is "falsely called knowledge" (*pseudonymou gnoseos,* 6:20) and often understood to refer to some form of gnostic or proto-gnostic thought. Those who "have already turned away to follow Satan" (5:15) may merely be widows or others who have chosen a different way of expressing their faith and may testify only to the author's penchant for demonizing everyone who disagrees with him about anything.

More interesting and unusual in documents where generalized polemic is the order of the day is the reference to specific dissidents, Hymenaeus and Alexander, who have "suffered shipwreck in their faith" and been "turned over to Satan" (1:19-20). Even if, as is likely, the letters are fictional, written pseudonymously in the name of Paul, it is quite possible that these names refer to real dissidents known in the author's day. If, with most interpreters, we connect them with those of the same name in 2 Timothy, we might retrieve more specific information about them. Alexander may be the same as Alexander the coppersmith in 2 Tim 4:14, but all we would learn from this is that he "strongly opposed our message." Hymenaeus and Philetus, on the other hand, are charged with a more specific error: they have "swerved from the truth by proclaiming that the resurrection has already taken place, and thus have destroyed the faith of some" (2 Tim 2:17-18). This conviction associates them closely with Gnostics, who believed that the benefits associated with resurrection had already been received at baptism or at the moment of enlightenment when *gnosis* was received (Irenaeus, *Haer.* 1.23.5, 2.31.2; cf. Tertullian, *Res.* 19.1–7; and the Nag Hammadi *Treatise on Resurrection*).[1] Since spiritual resurrection was available in the present, as devotees awakened from sleep or death, a future resurrection was redundant (cf. 1 Cor 15:12). They were already immortal by virtue of their incorporation into Christ and the church. Clearly at one time these teachers had been influential, but the implication is that at the time of writing, they had been excommunicated, "turned over to Satan, so that they may learn not to blaspheme" (1 Tim 1:20). The implication could be that their punishment—excommunication or some sort of sickness is usually surmised—was designed to rehabilitate rather than to destroy, but the wording is too vague to be sure.

An analogous situation arose when Paul recommended that an immoral man in Corinth be "handed over to Satan for the destruction of the flesh." It seems likely that Paul envisaged premature death rather than sickness, even though he hoped that in the end "his spirit may be saved" (1 Cor 5:1-5).[2] It is clear that the Corinthians, up to this point, had taken a more relaxed view of the situation than Paul, as it is clear that the dissidents in 2 Timothy had gained a hearing among some in Ephesus. This draws our attention to the delicate question of labeling, discussed in the first chapter. In 1 and 2 Timothy it seems that the

1. The same view is associated in the *Acts of Paul* with Demas and Hermogenes, who fall out with and eventually betray Paul (*Acts of Paul,* 311–14).

2. Compare Ananias and Sapphira in Acts 5, who are struck down for deceiving the Jerusalem leaders about their possessions. The punishment is sudden and final. Oropeza (2000) would want to include 1 Corinthians 10, but it speaks generally about the possibility of falling away and not about any specific instances of it.

author(s) considered the named dissidents to be defectors, but it is much less clear that either the dissidents or those sections of the community they worked in would have accepted the label. They could easily have seen themselves as the proponents of a different and more authentic version of the Christian message. Thus, from one perspective they could be considered to be apostates, but from another maybe not.

In these early Christian writings, we are dealing with conflicting visions of what Christian belief and practice involved. We do not need to define the precise shape of the dissidents' views to know that they would probably not have accepted the judgment that they had defected or placed themselves beyond the limits of the community. They presumably had a different definition of what those limits were.

It is generally thought that Christian allegiance was defined more in terms of belief than of practice; if so, defection would have been a less obvious and public affair than it was, for example, for Jews. Apart from attendance at Christian gatherings, there may, in some instances, have been little overt distinction between Christians and other members of society. In the absence of public recantation, which was probably rare (though cf. 1 Cor 12:3, "no one speaking by the Spirit of God ever says, 'Let Jesus be cursed'"), it would have been relatively easy to slip away inconspicuously from a Christian community. For those Jewish Christians who followed a Jewish lifestyle and continued their association with the synagogue, the situation would have been even less clear to an outside observer, since often the only thing that distinguished them from their fellow Jews was their christological beliefs. In some instances they may have been reluctant to confess their allegiance publicly—as with the secret believers whom some think can be identified in the Gospel of John (8:30-31; 12:42-43)—but whether they did so or not, a decision to sever their ties with Christianity could have been done discreetly and without fuss.[3]

As time went by, however, relations between synagogue and church began to shake down, and they became more clearly distinguished

3. Some might include Judas among the Christian apostates, though in fact he becomes the symbol of Jewish treason in later Christian tradition. But at most he "betrayed" Jesus, not Christianity. See further Maccoby (1992). Klassen (1996) argues that the whole notion of "betrayal" is a mistake.

entities. One effect of this may be found in the oblique comments of the author of Hebrews to his readers:

> For it is impossible to restore again to repentance those who have once been enlightened, and have tasted the heavenly gift, and have shared in the Holy Spirit, and have tasted the goodness of the word of God and the powers of the age to come, and then have fallen away *(parapesontes)*, since on their own they are crucifying again the Son of God and are holding him up to contempt. (6:4-6; cf. 10:26-31)

> But recall those earlier days when, after you had been enlightened, you endured a hard struggle with sufferings, sometimes being publicly exposed to abuse and persecution, and sometimes being partners with those so treated. For you had compassion for those who were in prison and you accepted cheerfully the plundering of your possessions, knowing that you yourselves possessed something better and more lasting. (10:32-34)

Clearly there had been a problem with Christians who, in the eyes of the author, had reneged on their Christian commitment. They had already tasted the benefits of membership in the Christian community: knowledge of the truth, heavenly gifts, experience of the Spirit, and the goodness of God's word. Yet now they had fallen away and had—to use the unusually strong language of the author—spurned or recrucified the Son of God and made a mockery of his death. Repentance for such renegades is out of the question, and their punishment will be severe, even severer than the punishment of those who breach the Mosaic law (cf. "drifting away," 2:1; "falling short," 4:1). These defections appear to lie in the past at the time of writing; but, although the author expresses confidence in his readers (6:9), the issue is raised presumably because the possibility of a recurrence was not out of the question.

What led to the defections is not clear, but the allusions in 10:32-34 to past experiences of persecution, public harassment, confiscation, and imprisonment may be the best clue. Even so, a number of other things remain unclear. The persecution may have been instigated by Jews, and some think in terms of synagogue discipline (Harvey

1985:89), but there is no evidence that Jewish courts had the right to confiscate and imprison. More likely is an allusion to state harassment during the reign of Nero or Domitian.[4] The readers are commonly thought to have been Jewish Christians. The deep concern to establish the supersession of Jewish traditions, especially those related to the cult, together with the exhortation to "go to him [Jesus] outside the camp and bear the abuse he endured" (13:13), certainly suggest that the author is trying to wean his readers from a hankering after Jewish thought and practice. It is also possible that they were Gentiles who had previously formed an attachment to Judaism and were now wondering if they had left too much behind when they allied themselves with the Christians. Whether Jewish Christians or Gentile judaizers, these defectors probably, but not certainly, headed back to the Jewish community. If this reconstruction is correct, we may surmise that those who defected from the Christian community did so because of both persecution and an unsatisfied longing for aspects of the Judaism they had left, two motives that could have coincided and been mutually reinforcing. Whether they thought this meant that they had defected from the Christian community is not clear, though the author of Hebrews is in no doubt that it did.

A somewhat similar situation may have arisen in Asia Minor toward the end of the century as reflected in the book of Revelation:

> I know your affliction and your poverty, even though you are rich. I know the slander of those who say they are Jews and are not, but are a synagogue of Satan. Do not fear what you are about to suffer. Beware, the devil is about to throw some of you into prison so that you may be tested, and for ten days you will have affliction. But be faithful unto death and I will give you the crown of life. (Rev 2:9-10)

> I know that you have but little power, and yet you have kept my word and have not denied my name. I will make those of the synagogue of Satan who say that they are Jews and are not—I will make them come

---

4. The date (whether before or after 70 CE) and setting of Hebrews have been much discussed, but for our purposes they are not important. DeSilva (1996) likens apostasy to a client spurning a patron.

down and bow before your feet, and they will learn that I have loved you. (Rev 3:8-9)

The identification of those who "say they are Jews and are not" and the connection between this claim and the threat of persecution remain obscure. Many think they were the Jews of Smyrna and Philadelphia, the cities to which these statements are addressed, and that they had been involved in some way with the persecution of Christians. If so, the author is usually taken to be appropriating the title "Jew" for Christians—in effect claiming, "We are the true Jews." Even so it remains unclear why the author would, without further qualification, simply say that Jews are not Jews. Some therefore insist that the statement be taken literally: they are non-Jews who were claiming to be Jews. In this case, they were most likely to have been Gentile judaizers, that is, non-Jewish Christians who were attracted to and had begun to identify with Judaism (Wilson 1992:613–14).

The reason they had turned toward Judaism remains unclear. Perhaps they had previously been Jewish sympathizers before becoming Christians and were now returning to old habits and interests. But if we extrapolate from the general situation implied by the book—a beleaguered Christian community facing what was perceived to be a hostile Roman state—we may surmise that these Christians had turned to the synagogue as a haven from persecution.[5] In Roman eyes, Judaism was a better established and more acceptable tradition and may have offered a protective umbrella under which Christians could shelter. In the eyes of the author, however, seeking protection amounted to defection. The link between persecution and defection is not clearly spelled out anymore than is the similar situation that seems to be implied by the Epistle to the Hebrews. Yet it is not difficult to imagine that pressure from outside, which had already led to one martyrdom (Rev 2:13),

---

5. Revelation has in the past commonly been associated with persecution of Christians during the reign of Domitian. More recently it has been noted that the crisis may have been as much a matter of perception as of reality, and there has been a concerted attempt to rehabilitate the reputation of Domitian, including his policies toward Christians and Jews. So Thompson (1990:95–115), who, I think, swings the pendulum too far. For a more balanced assessment, see Jones (1992:114–25, 166–69) and J. T. Sanders (1993:166–69).

could have encouraged some Christians to turn to the synagogue for protection. If they had had a connection with the synagogue before joining the Christians, the move would have been all the more natural.

Another text that indicates that state harassment may have been a factor in apostasy is *Hermas,* which twice mentions apostates and considers their ultimate fate. In a complex parable, willow sticks given to those who had heard God's message and returned in varying conditions, from the green and budding to the dried and withered, symbolize different groups and different responses. Some of them are described as follows:

> "Listen," he [the shepherd] said, "Those whose sticks were found withered and eaten by grubs are the apostates and traitors *(apostatai kai prodotai)* to the church, who by their sins have blasphemed the Lord, and in addition were ashamed of the Lord's name by which you were called. These, therefore, utterly perished to God. And you see that not one of them repented, even though they heard the words which you spoke to them, which I commanded you. From men of this sort life has departed. But those who returned the withered and uneaten sticks are very close to them, for they were hypocrites and brought in strange doctrines, and perverted God's servants, especially the ones who had sinned, by not allowing them to repent, but dissuading them instead with their moronic doctrines. These, then, have the hope of repentance. And you see that many of them have indeed repented, and still more will repent. But those who will not repent have lost their life." (*Sim.* 8.6.4–6)[6]

In a subsequent parable about twelve mountains that personify twelve different sorts of believers, we find similar words:

> "From the first mountain, the black one, are believers such as these: apostates and blasphemers *(apostatai kai blasphemoi)* against the Lord, and betrayers *(prodotai)* of God's servants. For these there is no repentance, but there is death, and that is why they are black, for their

---

6. Translations of *Hermas* are by J. B. Lightfoot and J. R. Harmer, revised by M. W. Holmes (1992).

kind is lawless. And from the second mountain, the bare one, are the believers such as these: hypocrites and teachers of evil. These, then, are like the first in not having the fruit of righteousness. For as their mountain is without fruit, so also men such as these have the Name, but are devoid of faith, and there is no fruit of truth in them. To these, then, repentance is offered, if they repent quickly; but if they delay their death will be with the first group." "Why, sir," I said, "is there repentance for them but not for the first group? For their actions are almost the same." "This is why," he said, "repentance is offered to them: they have not blasphemed their Lord, nor become betrayers of God's servants. Yet because of the desire for gain they acted hypocritically, and each one taught to suit the desires of sinful men. But they will pay a penalty; yet repentance is offered to them, because they did not become blasphemers or betrayers *(blasphemoi, prodotai)*." (*Sim.* 9.19.1–3)

In both of these passages, the heavenly messenger draws a distinction between those who are utterly condemned—variously described as apostates, blasphemers and betrayers—and the "hypocrites" and "teachers of evil" for whom repentance is possible. Asked why, considering the similarity of their deeds, the messenger answers that the latter were not blasphemers or betrayers. Despite their false teaching, their discouragement of those who wished to repent (it would be helpful to know what this obscure allusion refers to), and their tendency to pander to their audience, they are still eligible for repentance. In a related passage, the double-minded who "worship idols because of their cowardice and are ashamed of the name of their Lord whenever they hear about a persecution" are also eligible for repentance, presumably because they also had neither blasphemed nor betrayed (*Sim.* 9.21.3).

"Apostasy" in these passages seems to be defined by specific actions implicit in the two other terms. "Blasphemy" reminds us of the sacrifice to pagan gods and cursing of Christ required of those denying Christian allegiance in Bithynia (Freudenberger 1969:147) and in the accounts of Christian trials from Polycarp on. "Betrayal" could in a general sense mean only that these former believers had abandoned their community, a mere synonym for defection. But given the importance placed on it by the author, as something that put them beyond the pale, it more likely means that they had become informers and had betrayed their fellow Christians to the Roman authorities (Jeffers 1991:129). Indeed, since the author can envisage repentance for the cowards who worship idols under pressure (above), blasphemy and betrayal must refer to something more heinous. Cursing Christ and informing on fellow believers are, moreover, two things we know about from other sources as well.

Hermas is usually thought to come from Rome some time in the second century, but Maier has made a good case for an earlier date.[7] The circumstances in which apostasy and betrayal occurred are not given, but two things are discussed that may shed some light on the matter. First, there are references to persecution, either past or to come (*Vis.* 2.2.7; 4.1.6–9; *Sim.* 8.6.4; 8.8.2), and we can recall again the statement that associates idol worship and betrayal precisely with times of persecution, referring to those who "worship idols because of their cowardice and are ashamed of the name of their Lord whenever they hear about a persecution" (*Sim.* 9.21.3). The allusions could be to events in the time of Domitian, the time of Pliny (see below), or any similar second-century situation in which Christians were publicly arraigned and required to confirm or deny their faith.

Second, denial and defection are often associated with the problem of riches, a recurrent theme of the book:

> But some of them fell away completely *(telos apestesan)*. These, there-fore, have no repentance, for on account of their business affairs they blasphemed the Lord and denied him. (*Sim.* 8.8.2)

> These are the ones who have faith, but also have the riches of this world. Whenever persecution comes, they deny their Lord because of their riches and their business affairs. (*Vis.* 3.6.5)

The same association is made elsewhere (*Sim.* 1.4–6; 6.2.3–4). Wealthy Christians, some of whom became wealthy as Christians (*Sim.* 8.9.1) and many of whom were probably benefactors and/or leaders of

---

7. Maier summarizes the options and argues for a date toward the end of the first century (1991:55–58).

the house churches, found themselves prised from the Christian community by their social and financial connections to the outside world and the pressure to live according to pagan standards (*Sim.* 8.8.1; 8.9.1–3; 9.20.2; *Man.* 10.1.4–5).[8] Some continued in the faith even if they did not do the works of faith, but others were absorbed entirely into their pagan environment:

> . . . those who had been faithful, but became rich and acquired a reputation among the pagans. They clothed themselves with great pride and became arrogant and abandoned the truth and did not associate with the righteous, but lived with and according to the standards of pagans, and this life-style was more pleasant to them. Yet they did not fall away from God, but continued in the faith, though they did not do the works of faith. Many of them, therefore, repented. . . . But others, living entirely among the heathen and being corrupted by the worthless opinions of the heathen, fell away from God and behaved like the heathen. These, therefore, were counted with the heathen. (*Sim.* 8.9.1–3; cf. 8.10.3)

The problems of the wealthy seem to have been constantly on the mind of the author, no doubt because assimilation was a constant temptation and in itself accounted for some of the defections. But the acid test often came in times of persecution. For while the Romans did not authorize any official or widespread persecution, when Christians were brought to their attention by informers or by their own activities, they were invariably faced with a stark option: confess and die or deny and live. In addition, the families stood to lose all their property through confiscation. For some of the wealthy and well connected, it seems, allegiance was too great a price to pay (*Vis.* 3.6.5 above). And

8. So Maier (1991:66–67). See also Lampe, who thinks *Hermas*'s notion of a second repentance and the concession that the rich can be involved in one business (rather than many) are designed to entice the rich back to the church and to ensure that the poor are taken care of (2003:90–99). It is probable that the author of *Hermas* had once been rich (2003:218–36), but was not so now (probably because of imprisonment and confiscation), so he knew some of the pressures firsthand. Jeffers (1991:171–72) separates the problems of apostasy and wealth.

when they defected, they may well have dragged other Christians into the limelight by betraying them to the authorities.

Hermas thus presents us with a quite rich array of material, albeit sometimes oblique. There were different degrees of assimilation among the wealthy, ranging from mere neglect of the Christian poor to total absorption in pagan life, the latter signifying that such people were beyond the pale even if they are not called "apostates" or "betrayers" in the text. There were also different degrees of denial under pressure, ranging from the merely hesitant who come through in the end (*Sim.* 9.28.4), through those who deny but can repent (when divested of their wealth, *Vis.* 3.6.5–6; *Sim.* 9.21.3), to those called "apostates"/"betrayers"/"blasphemers," whose uncompromising denial and betrayal of others seem to place them beyond redemption. It also highlights the effect that the pressures of family and friends, social status and threats from the ruling order could have on defection.

In a number of the instances included here, the evidence for defection is oblique. The setting and meaning of texts have to be reconstructed from elusive hints, and the point of view of the accusers (rather than the defectors) is dominant. Not all the evidence is as equivocal as this, and one aspect of the story—pressure from Roman authorities—is vividly described in Pliny the Younger's letter to Trajan about his treatment of Christians in Bithynia, written about 110–12 CE:

> I have never taken part in any examination of Christians, so I do not know what is the object of the investigation or the degree of punishment.
>
> I have had grave doubts whether there should be any distinction of ages or whether the young, however tender their years, should in no way be differentiated from the stronger; whether pardon should be granted to recantation or whether one who had been a complete Christian should have no benefit from having given it up; whether the name itself, if free from crime or abominations attached to the name, should be punished. Meanwhile I followed this method in dealing with those against whom information was laid.
>
> I asked them whether they were Christians. If they confessed it, I asked a second time and a third time and threatened punishment; if

they persisted, I ordered their execution. For I had no doubt that, whatever it was to which they confessed, their pertinacity and obstinacy ought certainly to be punished. There were others equally mad, whom I sent to Rome, because they were Roman citizens.

Presently, as proceedings were under way, the charge spread in a variety of forms. An anonymous pamphlet was published containing the names of many. If they denied that they were or had been Christians, when, saying after me, they called upon the gods and with offerings of wine and incense prayed to your statue, which for this reason I had ordered to be brought along with the images of the gods, if moreover they cursed Christ, none of which, it is said, can those who are truly Christians be forced to do, I thought that they should be let go.

Others named by an informer presently denied it, saying that they had indeed been Christians, but had stopped, some three years before, some several years before, a few even twenty years before. These also worshipped both your statue and the images of the gods and cursed Christ.

Moreover they asserted that this had been the sum total of their guilt or error, namely that on a fixed day it was their custom to meet before dawn, to sing a hymn by turns to Christ as God, and to bind themselves by oath, not to some crime, but not to commit theft or banditry or adultery, not to betray a trust, not to refuse return of a deposit if requested. After doing this they were in the habit of parting and coming together again for a meal, but food common and harmless; they had stopped doing this after my edict, by which, according to your instructions, I had banned clubs *(collegia)*.

I therefore thought it the more necessary to discover the truth there was in this by also putting to torture two slave girls, who were called ministrants. I found nothing but a degrading and extravagant superstition. I therefore postponed the examination and hastened to consult you. I thought the matter fit for consultation, chiefly because of the number of those endangered. For many of every age, of every rank, of both sexes too are being cited and will be cited to face the danger. The contagion of that superstition had spread not only to the cities but also through villages and the countryside; it seems that it can be checked and corrected.

> Certainly it is pretty well agreed that the temples by now almost deserted have begun to be thronged and sacred rites long neglected are being resumed and on every side the flesh of sacrificial victims is being sold, which up till now very rarely found a purchaser. From this it is easy to imagine what a host of people can be reclaimed if there is an opportunity for recantation. (*Ep.* 10:96–97, trans. Whittaker 1984:150–52)

This extraordinarily rich, but sadly all too rare, account of the interaction of Christians with the state can be used to shed light on the many other places where we are left with only hints and suggestions, such as in Hebrews or Revelation. Here we have a firsthand account written not by a Christian but by the Roman official involved directly in the case. We can note a number of things.

First, that despite any pressures they may have come under, Christians could thrive and grow. Pliny notes that they were many in number, men and women, and of every age and rank, sufficient that their influence led to neglect of the temples and disruption of the market for meat.

Second, that Christians typically presented a problem for Roman officials only when they were forced on their attention, usually by informers. The informers, especially when they remained anonymous, presented a problem that both Pliny and Trajan, in his reply, are alert to. Trajan insists that anonymous accusations alone are insufficient grounds for action, but it is clear that they could set the ball rolling and with sudden and devastating effect on those accused.

Third, the test of allegiance—honoring the gods and the emperor and cursing Christ—is the earliest account of what was to become the standard procedure for testing the faithful.

Fourth, that here, as in later trials, mere confession of allegiance (the "name" Christian) was sufficient to establish guilt. No other crime was required and, on the evidence of eager defectors and casually tortured slaves, Pliny admits that no other crime could be proven. He thus confirms from the Roman side a grievance repeatedly taken up by later Christian apologists—the injustice of persecution for confession of the "name" alone even though no other crime could be proven.

Finally, and for our purposes most interesting, Pliny mentions the reaction of three groups accused of Christian allegiance: those who unequivocally confessed and were summarily executed or, if citizens, sent to Rome; those who flatly denied it and were released; and those who admitted association in the past but not in the present. The last of these Pliny was inclined to release (and this may be why he emphasizes that Christians were not guilty of any crime other than confessing the name) if they agreed to sacrifice to the gods and the emperor and to curse Christ—a policy of which Trajan, in his reply, approved.[9]

This group, Pliny says, claimed that they had withdrawn from the Christian movement three, several, or even twenty years before. What precipitated their defection is unclear. The references to three and several years prior do not coincide with any known events, but then we have only scrappy information about Christianity at this time. Those who defected twenty years before could have done so in the reign of Domitian when, according to some traditions, Christians came under particular pressure. They may thus have defected in circumstances similar to those described by Pliny. Or it may be that in each case these people had quietly ceased their association in the past, for reasons now unknown, but were now forced for the first time into a public recantation. The impression given is that the defectors hastened to declare their allegiance and encouraged Pliny to take a lenient view of them by noting that being a Christian involved no crime other than allegiance.

Although we are not told how many defectors there were, they made up a sufficiently distinctive group for him to be exercised about their fate. His concern about the number and influence of Christians in general suggests that the defectors were also more than a mere handful, and he expresses the hope that in the future many will be reclaimed if the opportunity for recantation is provided.

Strictly speaking, this rare glimpse into the world of early Christians in conflict with the Roman government tells us only about Bithynia ca. 110 CE. But given the paucity of our sources on such

---

9. Freudenberger (1969:141–44) notes the parallel with the sacrifice required of Antiochus (Josephus, *War* 7.46–52) and of the Jews in the Maccabean period (1 Macc 1:43); the requirement of a curse, he notes, does not recur in later Christian trials.

matters, it is plausible to suppose that the experience was repeated in other places and at other times, even if we accept that Roman persecution of Christians was sporadic. And if this is so, we may suppose that defection was not as uncommon as we might otherwise think.

Whether any of these Christians thought they could secretly retain their beliefs despite their public recantation is not known. At a later date, some Christian leaders, like Pionius, viewed those who succumbed during times of persecution sympathetically and tried to comfort and correct them (Eusebius, *Hist. eccl.* 4.15.47). As we shall see, the evidence of Cyprian from a later date encourages us to raise these questions again.

It is appropriate at this point to move forward in time and consider some of the later Christian evidence that fills out the picture presented by Pliny.[10] In connection with the martyrdom of Polycarp, we read of Quintus:

> Now there was one Quintus by name, a Phrygian recently arrived from Phrygia, who, when he saw the wild beasts, turned coward. This was the man who had forced himself and some others to come forward voluntarily. The proconsul, after many appeals, finally persuaded him to swear the oath and to offer the sacrifice. For this reason therefore, brothers, we do not praise those who hand themselves over, since the gospel does not so teach. (*Mart. Pol.* 4, trans. Holmes 1992)

Quintus, it appears, at first eagerly volunteered for martyrdom and encouraged others to do likewise. Faced with the horrors that awaited martyrs, however, he reneged and, as Eusebius has it in his retelling of the story, "he abandoned his salvation" (*Hist. eccl.* 4.15.7–8). His willingness to swear the oath and offer the sacrifice is seen as a warning against precipitate confession. While early Christian writers generally supported acceptance of martyrdom, they often had to discourage those who too aggressively sought it and sometimes argued that fleeing to safety was justifiable. For example, Clement fled under pressure in 202–3 CE, and

10. The best discussions are Musurillo (1972) and Droge and Tabor (1992).

early in his career, Tertullian considered this a legitimate response—though he later changed his mind.[11] It is reported that Basilides, the renowned gnostic Christian, thought there was no harm in eating idol food or lightly denying the faith during times of persecution (Eusebius, *Hist. eccl.* 4.7.7), though this seems more like a temporary ploy (like flight) than a genuine defection. He seems to have distinguished between outward action and inner conviction. Eusebius reports that during the persecutions at Lyons and Vienne under Marcus Aurelius, some defected, but he prefers to dwell on those who retracted their denial (*Hist. eccl.* 5.1.11, 25, 32–35, 45–48). In the *Martyrdom of Pionius,* it is recorded that there were deserters (10.5–6, 12.2, 20.3), some of whom voluntarily offered sacrifice (4.3) and others of whom, like the leader Euctemon, tried unsuccessfully to persuade the rest to follow them (15.2; 16.1; 18.13–14; Musurillo 1972:137–67).

Our richest source is Cyprian's *De Lapsis,* in which he defends his rigorist line on dealing with the "lapsed" who had succumbed during the Decian persecution in 250–51 CE, but who subsequently wanted to return to the church. In the course of this argument, he gives a vivid picture of the behavior of Christians in Carthage, where he was the newly appointed bishop. In an attempt to encourage unity and the honoring of traditional gods, the Romans required a public confession that involved sacrifice to pagan gods in front of a usually "scoffing crowd" (28.15–20; cf. 2.8–17). He describes a number of groups, the first of which was the confessors, some of whom were martyred, some of whom survived their torture and returned to the church, whether men, women, virgins or boys (chaps. 2–3). Closely allied was the second group, the ordinary faithful *(stantes),* who were not cowed by the pending fight and would have stood firm but were saved at the last minute by the cessation of persecution: "Rooted unshakably in the laws of God and disciplined in the teachings of the gospel, they were unmoved by fear at the decrees of banishment, at the tortures awaiting them, or the threats against their property and persons" (2.23–34). A third group consisted of the fugitives, people like Cyprian himself, who went into hiding, had their property confiscated, but made no public denial (chaps. 3, 4, 10).

11. Droge and Tabor (1992:140–52) summarizing Clement of Alexandria, Tertullian, and Origen.

Cyprian was somewhat defensive about his decision since, in the eyes of some, going into hiding was not equal to public confession. In what is doubtless a strongly autobiographical passage, he concedes the primacy of confession but insists that flight comes a close second on the scale of faithful reactions:

> Once the period prescribed for apostatizing *(dies negantibus praseti-tutus)* had passed, whoever had failed to declare himself within the time thereby confessed that he was a Christian. If the primary claim to victory is that, having fallen into the hands of the pagans, a man should confess the Lord, the next title to glory is that he should have gone underground and preserved himself for further service of the Lord. The first makes a public confession, the second a private one; the first wins a victory over an earthly judge, the second is content to have God as his judge and keeps his conscience unsullied by his integrity of heart; in the first, courage is more active; in the second, conscientiousness has inspired prudence. The former, when his hour came, was found to be ripe for it; for the other it was perhaps only a postponement: he abandoned his estate and went into hiding because he was not going to deny his faith; indeed he intended to confess, should he be arrested after all. (3.1–14)[12]

On the other end of the spectrum were the potential *lapsi,* those who considered denial but were not required to make a decision, but who later needed to confess to a priest to ease their guilty conscience (28.1–7). Then there were the apostates. The first group are called the *libellatici,* those who got a false certificate of sacrifice through bribery:

> Nor let people flatter themselves that they need do no penance because they have kept their hands clean from the impious sacrifices, when all the time certificates of sacrifice have polluted their conscience. Why, such a certificate is itself a confession of apostasy *(professio denegantis),* it is a testimonial that the Christian has renounced what he once was. (27.1–5)

---

12. Excerpts are from the translation of Bévenot (1971).

Cyprian seems offended as much by their lack of guilt as by their evasive action. While they seem to have thought that they had come out unscathed, he labels them apostates, illustrating the disjunction between the perceptions of labeler and labeled that we have noticed elsewhere.

That disjunction would have been less apparent with the *sacrificati*, those who acceded to the pressure to sacrifice to pagan gods (chaps. 7–9). Many of these, Cyprian ruefully notes, rushed to offer sacrifice before they were arrested. They were not forced against their will; rather, they eagerly pressured the magistrates to let them sacrifice at once.

> But many were not satisfied with their own destruction: they encouraged one another and rode to their ruin in a body; with poisoned cup they toasted each other's death. And to crown this accumulation of crimes: parents even carried their babies and led their youngsters to be robbed of what they had received in earliest infancy. (9.1–5)

Egging one another on and dragging their children with them, these defectors swept up many in their path. These are the "apostates and renegades" mentioned later in the letter (*apostati, perfidis*, 33.16), presumably the ones who did not come back. Some surely did come back, since it is the conditions for their return to the church that are at the heart of the dispute between the rigorists and the moderates. Cyprian defends his hard line against the more accommodating approach of surviving confessors, though his own flight must have placed him in a relatively weak position, and he was later to soften his views in the face of a devastating plague and the threat of new persecutions. At any rate, some of the lapsed later wished to recant their public defection and return to the church. Defection, that is, was not necessarily final.

If we stand back from his own strong-minded views, Cyprian indirectly suggests a number of insights into the motives and processes of defection in the face of official state harassment. The sheer brutality of the process would sometimes be enough to overcome those struggling to remain faithful (12). In some places the impression given is that ties to friends and protection of families had a profound effect, despite Cyprian's caustic way of presenting things (9.1). In others he sees evidence of a church gone slack, things that, reading between the lines, point to dilemmas that would have been pressing and real. For example, marriage to a pagan spouse would have created intense conflicts in times of persecution (6); the accumulation of property and wealth and fear for its loss were also strong motives for defection (11–12). Here we begin to see that defection was rarely a simple matter, a case of retaining or abandoning religious convictions. Rather, those convictions were inexorably tied to the familial and social context of the people concerned.

As we saw above, some allusions to defection, such as those in Hebrews and Revelation, seem to imply some sort of connection between defection and persecution. In other places we have hints that Christians defected without the pressure of an external threat. *1 Clement* may suggest this, although the allusions are admittedly fleeting and obscure:

> In this way the Master clearly demonstrated that he does not forsake those who hope in him, but destines to punishment and torment those who turn aside *(tous heteroklineis hyparchontes)*. Of this his [Lot's] wife was destined to be a sign, for after leaving with him she changed her mind and no longer agreed, and as a result she became a pillar of salt to this day, that it might be known to all that those who are double-minded and those who question the power of God fall under judgment and become a warning to all generations. (11:1–2, trans. Holmes 1992)

Jeffers (1991:173) has suggested that the double-minded who doubt God's power are the same as those accused of rebelling against the elders in 47:7, and that they may have been converts from Judaism who had returned to the synagogue and turned against the Christians. This is possible, though it depends on broader assumptions about the setting and purpose of the text.

A series of allusions in the letter of *Barnabas* are more specific and provide some clues about the author, the recipients, and a group in the community that the author opposes:

> So for this reason, brothers, he who is very patient, when he saw how the people whom he had prepared in his beloved would believe in all

purity, revealed everything to us in advance, in order that we might not shipwreck ourselves by becoming, as it were, "proselytes" to their law. (3:6)

Before we believed in God, our heart's dwelling-place was corrupt and weak, truly a temple built by human hands, because it was full of idolatry and was the home of demons, for we did whatever was contrary to God. (16:7)

Do not continue to pile up your sins while claiming that the covenant is both theirs and ours, because those people lost it completely in the following way, when Moses had just received it. (4:6)

Now the Scripture says, "Not unjustly are the nets spread out for the birds." This means that a man deserves to perish if, having knowledge of the way of righteousness, he ensnares himself in the way of darkness. (5:4)[13]

The first two passages suggest that both the author and the recipients were Gentiles, and that some of the community members were judaizing. The third passage, which it is natural to connect with the others, indicates the presence of those who took the view that God's covenant was shared by Jews and Christians alike—a highly unusual view in Christian circles of the day. It is apparently the same group whom the author describes as those who have known but abandoned Christian truth (5:4). Against the flow of Christian opinion (including that of the author), in which Judaism was seen to be inferior to and entirely distinct from Christianity, the judaizers claimed that the two were on equal footing, joint heirs of a covenant within which they could peacefully coexist. There is no mention of hostile pressure from the state. Rather, there is evidence elsewhere in the letter that a Roman government sympathetic to Jewish ambitions, especially their desire to rebuild the Jerusalem Temple, may have encouraged a resurgence of hope and confidence among Jews. This, in turn, would have made them more attractive and thus, for Christians, a force to be reckoned with. It

13. Translation by Holmes (1992).

is this—Roman support for the Jews rather than Roman opposition to Christians—that is the more likely context in which these judaizing Christians developed their "shared covenant" theory. In the eyes of the author, they are defectors—they have known the truth but have abandoned it. The judaizers, of course, may well have seen things very differently, though we are not told how they now viewed their position in the Christian community.[14]

Another snippet of evidence comes from Justin's discussion of the relationships among various Jewish-Christian groups, Gentile Christians and the synagogue communities (*Dial.* 46–47). Justin is taxed by Trypho about the fate of Christians who continue to keep the Jewish law, and, admitting that others are of a different view, he declares that Jewish Christians who keep the law and do not impose it on Gentile Christians will be saved (47:1–2). As to others, he says:

> "But those of your [Jewish] race, Trypho," I said, "who say they believe in this Christ, but compel the Gentiles who believe in this Christ to live completely according to the law ordained by Moses, or do not choose close fellowship with them, likewise such men as these I do not accept. But I suppose that even those [Gentiles] who were persuaded by them to join the legal community, together with observing the confession of the Christ of God, that those will be saved likewise. I do declare, however, that those will never be saved who have confessed and come to know this man [Jesus] to be the Christ, but have for some reason switched *(metabaino)* and joined the legal community, now denying that he is the Christ and not changing their mind before their death." (*Dial.* 47:3–4, trans. Betz 1979:335)

The clear reference to erstwhile Christians who had defected to the synagogue and openly denied their Christian beliefs is unusual. It is just possible that these were Jewish Christians, but the flow of Justin's statement, plus the suggestion that they had "switched" rather than "returned" to the synagogue, suggests that they were Gentiles. We are

---

14. For further discussion of the possible interpretations of *Barnabas,* including the textual variant in 4:6, see Wilson (1995:127–42, 160–61).

not told what motivated them, only that they defected "for some reason," but the general context suggests that a significant role was played by Jewish persuasion.[15] If so, we gain a glimpse of yet another element in the process of defection—active enticement from another quarter, in this case Judaism.

A quite different and unusual set of circumstances faced the Jewish Christians who got caught up in the Bar Kokhba rebellion and whose divided loyalties led them to run foul of the political forces of the day. Justin mentions that some of them were put to death for refusing to recognize the claims of Bar Kokhba: "In the Jewish war which happened just recently, Bar Kokhba, the leader of the Jewish revolt, ordered that Christians alone should be led away to terrible punishments, unless they would deny Jesus the Messiah and blaspheme" (*1 Apol.* 31.6; cf. *Dial.* 16; cf. Eusebius, *Hist. eccl.* 4.6.2).

To this we may add the fascinating, if obscure, *Apocalypse of Peter,* which has been persuasively dated to the period 132–35 CE and seen as a response to the crisis faced by Jewish Christians during the Bar Kokhba rebellion.[16] A date before 135 seems likely since Bar Kokhba's defeat is not mentioned, as it surely would have been if it had been known. For the author, the crisis is a sign of the imminent end when the martyrs will be redeemed and God's true people revealed, a theme whose details are extensively explored in chapters 4–17. It is chapters 1–2, however, that are crucial to understanding the setting. Bauckham (1985; 1998) shows that the first two chapters are an adaptation of select parts of Matthew 24, that the teaching is attributed to the risen (not the earthly) Jesus, and that it is specifically targeted at the generations that came after the apostles ("those who come after us," 1:1). The overriding concern is the issue of false messiahship, revealed in the shift from a concern with "messiahs" (chap. 1) to a "messiah" (chap. 2), and in the insistence that the coming of Christ will be universally visible, unlike the obscure appearances of false messiahs (cf. also chap. 17). Further details are suggested in the following obscure words:

15. For further discussion, see Wilson (1992:609–10).

16. The most interesting discussions are in Buchholz (1988) and Bauckham (1985; 1998), the last providing a convenient summary of his longer surveys in 1988 and 1994.

(8) They will promise that "I am the Christ who has come into the world." And when they see the wickedness of his deed they will turn away after them. (9) And they will deny him to whom our fathers gave praise whom they crucified, the first Christ, and sinned exceedingly. But this liar is not Christ. And when they have rejected him he will kill with the sword and many will become martyrs. . . . (11) This is the house of Israel only. They will be martyrs by his hand. . . . (12) For Enoch and Elijah will be sent that they might teach them that this [is] the Deceiver who must come into the world and do signs and wonders and deceive. (13) And on account of this those who die by his hands will be martyrs and will be reckoned with the good and righteous martyrs who have pleased God in their life. (2:8–13, trans. Buchholz 1988)

Buchholz (1988:283–89, 408–12) understands these words as follows: some, presumably Jewish, Christians (v. 11) joined the cause of the false messiah (v. 8), which amounted to a denial of Christ (v. 9); when they realized that he was not the messiah, they abandoned him and he in turn persecuted and killed them (vv. 10–11); messengers are promised who will confirm that he is the deceiver and that these are the end times (v. 12); and the one-time defectors, now martyrs, will be counted among the righteous (v. 13). This is an attractive interpretation that helps to flesh out Justin's laconic notice mentioned above: the Christians caught up in the Bar Kokhba rebellion were Jewish Christians; and they were persecuted not just because they were Christians but because they had supported and then abandoned Bar Kokhba. Initially attracted to him, they eventually balked at accepting him as the messiah. If this is correct, the Christians were in the eyes of the author guilty of a double defection: first, by supporting the Bar Kokhba movement and denying Christ; and second, by subsequently denying that Bar Kokhba was the messiah, abandoning the rebellion and, presumably, returning to their Christian communities. However, the allusions in chapter 2 are obscure and this is not the only way they can be understood.

Bauckham thinks the sequence may be "that at first the Antichrist [Bar Kokhba] would command the support of the majority of Jews, who would recognize him as the messiah and thereby continue to deny the Messiah Jesus, though the faithful Jewish Christian minority would reject the Antichrist and suffer martyrdom. Then Enoch and Elijah would come to expose the Antichrist as a deceiver, with the result that many Jews would then reject him and be put to death by him as martyrs" (1985:283). Bauckham nevertheless finds an allusion to Christian apostates among those tortured in hell—those who blasphemed and betrayed "the way of righteousness," that is, Christianity—as well as to those who betrayed and persecuted them (chaps. 7 and 9). Buchholz's interpretation seems closer to the flow of the text, but then the text is not transparent and its meaning is obscured by the material that surrounds it.[17] At any rate, we seem in one place or another in the text to have an allusion to Christian apostates.

What precisely took place and why is not clear. Christians who initially supported Bar Kokhba may not have seen it as a denial of Christ. At first they may have thought that they were merely supporting a Jewish liberation movement, and it may have been precisely the pressure to recognize Bar Kokhba's messianic status that led to their withdrawal and subsequent execution. Other evidence suggests that Bar Kokhba rigorously upheld the law and was ruthless with those who opposed him, and this suggests that there was nothing out of character in his reported action against Christians.[18] It was rare for divisions within Judaism to turn so critically on questions of messiahship and even rarer for Christian Jews to be treated so severely by other Jews. But the passions and tensions aroused by the rebellion, and the temporary overthrow of Roman rule in a small part of Judea, produced a situation

---

17. Bauckham's interpretation seems to involve taking the "they" of vv. 8b and 9a to be non-Christian Jews who follow Bar Kokhba (and thus will not follow Christ), and the "they" of 9b as those Christians who reject Bar Kokhba and are killed. The change of subject is sudden, and it is easier to give the same sense to "they" throughout. As Bauckham (1985:284) himself points out, the fig tree parables that open chapter 2 do not help much since they can be read in more than one way, though he thinks that there is an allusion to the conversion of Jews to Christ either during or after the rule of the Antichrist (also Bauckham 1998:231). In addition to the conflict over Bar Kokhba's messianic claims, there may have been a rift between the rebels' desire to rebuild the Temple and the Christian claim that the true heavenly temple was already prepared for them (chap. 16; Bauckham 1998:232–33).

18. Bauckham (1985:286); Wilson (1995:6).

in which both the definition and the punishment of defection took an unusual turn.

Later in the century, Peregrinus, the publicity-hungry philosopher lampooned by Lucian, pursued his fascinating career. Peregrinus also went under the name "Proteus," which Lucian sarcastically suggests was appropriate in view of his constant transformations. According to Lucian, he was an adulterer and a corrupter of youth who had to leave his homeland after killing his father. He turned up in Palestine and joined the Christian movement:

> It was then that he learned the wondrous lore of the Christians, by associating with their priests and scribes in Palestine. And—how else could it be?—in a trice he made them all look like children, for he was prophet, cult-leader, head of the synagogue, and everything, all by himself. He interpreted and explained some of their books and even composed many, and they revered him as a god, made use of him as a lawgiver, and set him down as a protector, next after that other, to be sure, whom they still worship, the man who was crucified in Palestine because he introduced this new cult into the world.
>
> Then at length Proteus was apprehended for this and thrown into prison, which itself gave him no little reputation as an asset for his future career and the charlatanism and notoriety-seeking that he was enamored of. Well, when he had been imprisoned, the Christians, regarding the incident as a calamity, left nothing undone in the effort to rescue him. Then, as this was impossible, every other form of attention was shown him, not in any casual way but with assiduity, and from the very break of day aged widows and orphan children could be seen waiting near the prison, while their officials even slept inside with him after bribing the guards. Then elaborate meals were brought in, and sacred books of theirs were read aloud, and excellent Peregrinus—for he still went by that name—was called by them "the new Socrates." Indeed, people came even from the cities in Asia, sent by the Christians at their common expense, to succor and defend and encourage the hero. They show incredible speed whenever any such public action is taken; for in no time they lavish their all. So it was then in the case of Peregrinus; much money came to him from them by reason of his imprisonment, and he procured not a little revenue from it. (*Peregr.* 11–14)

He left home, then, for the second time, to roam about, possessing an ample source of funds in the Christians, through whose ministrations he lived in unalloyed prosperity. For a time he battened himself thus; but then, after he had transgressed in some way even against them—he was seen, I think, eating some of the food that is forbidden them—they no longer accepted him. (*Peregr.* 16)[19]

Lucian's satirical account of Peregrinus's remarkable and rapid rise to fame in Palestinian Christian circles, where he became "prophet, cult-leader, and head of the synagogue," presents him as an unprincipled opportunist and the Christians as gullible simpletons. His learning and literary skills singled him out and helped promote his reputation as "the new Socrates," even as a god second only to Christ. By whom and for what reason he was imprisoned is not stated, but presumably it had something to do with Christian allegiance. At any rate, it served only to enhance his reputation among Christians. Eventually things turned sour and he ran into difficulties for eating forbidden foods—probably those associated with pagan sacrificial rites (cf. Acts 15, 20, 29; Rev 2:14). So he defected, though as Lucian tells it, the Christians eased him out. Having left the Christians, he went to Egypt for ascetic training and returned to Italy a Cynic, promoting a blend of Cynicism and popular religion. Expelled from Italy, he ended up in Athens, where eventually, egged on by his followers, he publicly demonstrated his indifference to death in an act of self-immolation on a gigantic pyre. Soon after, an oracle and statues were established in his memory.

Of course, we need to dig beneath Lucian's caustic account in which Peregrinus is never given the benefit of the doubt, his every motive is suspect, and his every action designed for self-glorification. Some think Lucian was woefully ignorant about Christianity, that he confused it with the mystery cults, and that he did not know the difference between Christians and Jews. Interestingly, Christian writers who allude to Peregrinus as a pagan martyr do not mention his Christian phase (Tertullian, *Mart.* 4.5; Tatian, *Or. Graec.* 25.1; Athenagoras, *Leg.* 26.2–4), so that some are not sure whether, in his attempt to pillory both the philosophical charlatan and the gullible Christians, Lucian

---

19. Trans. A. M. Harmon (1936).

merely gave prominence to Peregrinus's Christian experience or simply invented the whole thing (Edwards 1989:92–93, 98). Certainly some of the details are implausible—that Christians treated Peregrinus as a god, or that he was head of a Christian "synagogue"—but other elements are not so far-fetched. The attractions of a Cynic to aspects of Christian gnomic wisdom and the lifestyle modeled by Jesus, the effect of an educated (possibly charismatic) pagan convert on an impressionable Christian community, and Christian support for a convert in trouble are all plausible details of the story. That Christians do not mention Peregrinus's defection is not surprising since it does not reflect too well on them. And if we accept that satire works best when it is at least partially based on fact, there is no reason to dismiss the broad outline of Lucian's version, namely that Peregrinus was both a convert to and a defector from Christianity. We shall never know what his motives were in either case, but it is probably safe to assume that they were a lot more complex than Lucian wants us to believe. With respect to his defection, we are told only that it hinged on his consumption of idol food. Perhaps this was the result of a difference of opinion whose consequences he did not fully understand (Christians after all did not concur on the issue); perhaps the once gullible Christians began to suspect that he was not the genuine convert they had taken him to be; or perhaps Lucian is right and Peregrinus was an egomaniac who obsessively sought the limelight as he moved from place to place. One or more of these could have been the precipitating factor. We may never know.

Toward the end of the third century, Porphyry produced one of the most acute and influential attacks on Christianity, *Against the Christians*. He had already broached the subject in an earlier work, *On the Philosophy from Oracles,* but in the later work, he relentlessly probes Christian tradition (especially biblical tradition) for contradictions and implausible historical and philosophical claims. No other anti-Christian work hit such a raw nerve, and after Constantine the work was so effectively banned by successive Christian emperors that only fragments have survived. Clearly Porphyry knew Christian traditions well, and some attribute that to his earlier allegiance to the church. One source claims that he was once a Christian but abandoned Christianity after receiving a beating by Christians (Socrates, *Hist. eccles.* 3.23.37–39). Some take this at face value, while others see it as a concoction to explain his later anti-Christian views. The least we can conclude is that he was close enough to Christianity to know it well, and one recent study suggests that he had a Christian background and was once well disposed to the movement as a whole (Kinzig 1998). What is meant by a "beating" is obscure (a verbal beating, some say), and whether his criticisms precipitated or later justified his defection remains obscure.[20]

If Porphyry was not himself a defector—and the evidence for this is weak—he nevertheless tells us about someone who was, a philosopher called Ammonius. He describes him as follows: "a Christian brought up in Christian ways by his parents, but when he began to think philosophically, he promptly changed his way of life conformably to the laws [i.e., pagan way of life]" (Eusebius, *Hist. eccl.* 6.19.9). Porphyry makes the point that whereas Ammonius's former student, Origen, was brought up and educated as a Greek but became a Christian, Ammonius himself went in the other direction. Eusebius refutes Porphyry's observation by claiming that Origen was brought up as a Christian and that Ammonius never ceased to be one (*Hist. eccl.* 6.19.10). This difference of opinion may be because there was more than one Ammonius and, possibly, more than one Origen. The Ammonius who taught Origen may not have been the same as the important Neoplatonist of the same name, but there is no reason to doubt Porphyry's claim that he was a defector from Christianity.[21] The laconic statement recorded by Eusebius tells us only that the more Ammonius learned of philosophy the less he was involved with Christianity—presumably a defector who was driven away by intellectual dissatisfactions.

Sometime in the fourth century an anonymous upper-class Christian senator was castigated for transferring his allegiance to pagan

20. Further on Porphyry's attack on Christianity, see Wilken (1984:126–63). He does not think Porphyry was ever a Christian.

21. There is reason to think that the renowned Neoplatonist, Ammonius, teacher of Plotinus, was not the same as the Neoplatonist Christian philosopher who taught Origen. To confuse things further, there may have been a Neoplatonist Origen who was not the same as the Christian Origen. See Edwards (1993:169–81). Schroeder (1987:495–506) argues that the Christian Ammonius did not defect but merely joined a marginal Christian sect.

gods and their cults (Pseudo-Cyprian, *Carmen ad Senatorum*).[22] The author is dumbfounded that someone who has tasted the truth of Christianity and held significant public offices could turn to pagan gods and their absurd rites:

> And the general rumour abroad had reached our ears that you have said: "Goddess, I was mistaken, forgive me, I have returned." Tell me, if you please, since you often made these requests and sought forgiveness, what words does she say to you? You, who follow those who are mindless, are truly deprived of your wits. Once again you seek out these things and do not realize that you are doing wrong. See what you deserve. Perhaps you would have been less notorious if you had only known this and persisted in this error. Yet, since you have crossed the threshold of the true Law and come to know God for a few years, why do you cling to what should be abandoned or why do you give up what should be retained? (lines 35–46)

It is implied that the senator was originally pagan, that he had converted to Christianity but had now abandoned it and returned to his pagan roots. It would have been better (and more understandable), says the author, if he had not converted in the first place, but simply persisted in his erroneous pagan ways. Still, all may not be lost, since mature old age and experience, it is hoped, may help him see the error of his ways and prompt a return to the Christian fold (lines 75–80).

There are details we would like to know about his conversion to and defection from Christianity, but they are not given. He may have been one of those who, in the period of transition from a pagan to a Christian empire, never fully gave up pagan habits when he became a Christian and thus found the switch back to paganism quite easy. A better fit might be with those whose conversion was nominal, a means of gaining advantage or preferment in a society increasingly inclined to favor Christians. His defection might even be associated with the reign of Julian the Apostate, when pagan ways were once again in vogue.[23] By

22. The text in translation is to be found in Croke and Harries (1982:84–85). The full title is "Poem to a Senator converted from Christianity to the service of idols."

23. MacMullen (1984:144–48; 1997:55–57) vividly describes the different types of allegiance to Christianity.

expressing hope that the defection may be reversed, the author suggests that it may have been a temporary aberration—but that is his, and not necessarily the senator's, perception. All we can say is that paganism was sufficiently attractive or advantageous for him to revert to his former ways.

Mention of Julian turns our attention toward the most notorious apostate of Late Antiquity. His father was the half-brother of Constantine, and Julian served as junior Caesar under the thumb of his cousin Constantius for six years (355–61 CE) before briefly becoming sole emperor in 361–63. During most of that time, he was constrained by the newly christianized imperial court. It was only in the last year or so that he was able publicly to express his change of allegiance, but when exactly he began to turn in that direction has been a matter of debate. Julian himself dates his defection from the time he was about twenty (ca. 351/352 CE). Writing some twelve years after the event— and thus with all the benefits and distortions of hindsight—Julian urges the Christians in Alexandria to reconsider their commitment:

> Heed my advice, and guide yourselves a little toward the truth: for you shall not err from the right path if you heed one who walked on that other path [of yours] until his twentieth year, but who is now in his twelfth year of walking this [right] path I speak of in the company of the gods. (Julian, *Ep.* 47)[24]

This is the clearest autobiographical allusion we have, and from it we learn something of the timing and of the radical nature of this change, but little about the factors that precipitated it. As a result—as with the conversion in the opposite direction of his famous uncle, Constantine—the causes and consequences of Julian's defection have provoked considerable speculation. As A. D. Nock has noted, Julian's defection (i.e., his "conversion" away from Christianity), with its emphasis on a new and exclusive adherence that reflects an either/or choice between Christianity and paganism, is more in line with Jewish and Christian concepts of religious allegiance than with those typical of the pagan world (Nock 1933:156–63). There is little reason to doubt the genuineness of Julian's commitment to Christianity in

24. The translation here and of Libanius (below) are from Smith (1995:182–83).

his youth, though no certain way of knowing when doubts first began to appear.[25]

Any attempt to probe the psychological roots of Julian's defection is frustrated by the lack of evidence as well as the inherent difficulty in getting inside someone's mind. But we can point to one or two things that probably had a bearing on the issue. The first is the political context in which he grew up and, in particular, the death of his father, half-brother, and other family members, and his own exile, all at the instigation of his cousin, the emperor Constantius. Machinations in the imperial court were not uncommon, especially in times of transition and succession, but the devastating results for Julian's immediate family may well have turned him against the new imperial religion and those who proclaimed it, despite his extensive Christian education and upbringing.

If such events turned him against Christianity, the sheer attractiveness of paganism—in the form of Neoplatonic philosophy, sacrificial cult, or theurgic initiation—seems to have played their part too. His contemporary, Libanius, in a speech written in 362 CE at Julian's request, declares:

> For there was hidden in that place a spark *[spinther]* of prophecy that had barely escaped the hands of the impious. As a result, Sire, you were soothed by the prophecies as you first began to seek out the hidden lore and you held in check your excessive hatred *[sphodron misos]* of the gods. And upon your arrival in Ionia you encountered a wise man *[sophos]*, you heard of those who fashion and maintain the universe, you gazed upon the beauty of philosophy and tasted its sweetest springs. Then you quickly threw aside your error, released yourself from darkness and grasped truth in place of ignorance, reality in place of falsehood, our old gods in place of that recent one and his wicked rites. (Libanius, *Orationes* 13.11–12)

This clearly implies that despite his "hatred of the gods" (i.e., Christian belief), Julian remained open to the appeal of philosophy and magical

25. Cook (2002:279–80) follows several earlier scholars in arguing that Julian's commitment was never more than skin-deep. Contrast Smith (1995:182–83). Wilken (1984:164–205) has a succinct overview of Julian's career.

lore. The former had long been part of his education, but his interest had intensified during 348–51 CE while he was staying in Nicomedia, Pergamum, and Ephesus. It was in Ephesus that he apparently underwent an initiation at the hands of one Maximus, a theurgic expert and avid Neoplatonist. It was a profound experience, a sort of conversion, that appears to have been critical in revealing the attractions of paganism. For Julian, pursuit of philosophy and worship of the gods, the rational and the emotional, went hand in hand.[26] In a virulent anti-Christian work, *Against the Galileans*, written just before his death, Julian is deeply motivated by "the indifference of Christians to the cult worship of the ancestral gods, and . . . their assumption that they could participate in the Greek republic of letters and yet deny what he saw as its religious core" (Smith 1995:207). But if it is true that the apostate Julian had a "polytheistic sensibility," it is not clear when this was formed—in his Christian or his pagan years, or in both. Likewise, his many dissatisfactions with Christianity that come to expression in *Against the Galileans* may have been niggling away for a long time, but how far back they go we cannot be sure. All we can say is that there was something personal and political in his rejection of Christianity, perhaps tied more to its representatives than to the system itself, and something both mystical and philosophical that drew him into another world. It is interesting to note that the man who would forever after be known as "the apostate" himself used exactly the same term to describe those noble (Christian) souls who submit themselves to pagan truths and "abandon atheism" (*Ag. Gal.* 384–85; Wright 1923). "Apostasy" was apparently, for Julian, precisely the right way to describe the transition from Christianity to paganism.

26. Contra Nock, who ascribes Julian's defection as being the outcome of an emotional rather than an intellectual quest (1933:157). Whether one precipitated the other and which one that was we shall never know. Smith provides a lengthy and thorough discussion of Julian's apostasy from Christianity and "conversion" to paganism (1995:179–218).

4

PAGAN DEFECTORS

This chapter will necessarily be shorter than the previous two. Some might suggest that it should not be here at all. The absence from Greco-Roman culture of the principle of exclusive commitment or firm boundaries that characterized Jewish and Christian communities (even if the reality was somewhat different) might seem to exclude the notion of defection or apostasy at the outset. In the context of the relaxed syncretism typical of so much of pagan society, apostasy or defection is an issue that does not immediately spring to mind. Yet we do find examples that look very much like the phenomena we have already uncovered in Jewish and Christian circles. True, the evidence rarely allows us to discuss them as fully as we would like, and that may be an indication that the phenomena were of less moment. But before we draw that conclusion, we need to see what evidence there is.

Burkert (1982) argues that the Pythagoreans had a strong sense of communal identity and that their members, both men and women, were committed to special rules for daily and cultic activity that separated them from other people. He notes a number of instances in which members of the early movement were ritually excluded for failing to fulfill their obligations or for betraying the cause. Failed novitiates were declared "dead," as were the reprobates who eventually overthrew

Pythagorean rule at Croton (Iamblichus, *VP* 73–74, 252). Empedocles was found guilty of stealing Pythagoras's teachings and excluded from the community (Diog. L. 8.54), and those who betrayed mathematical secrets died by drowning because of divine wrath (Iamblichus, *VP* 252). Noting that Pythagoreanism comes closer to the phenomenon of a sect than any other pre-Hellenistic movement, Burkert (1982:18) comments: "To establish facts with any confidence seems impossible. But the very idea is remarkable or even unique in the Greek world: ritual exclusion from the community in the most adamant form, by irrevocable death." The Pythagoreans have been described as the most authority-bound of the philosophical schools, treating the teaching of their founder as nearly infallible.[1] Thus those who betrayed the secret teachings were a type of defector, since they were presumably consciously defying the rules around which their community was structured. This evidence is, however, rather early for us, and while the later revivals of Pythagoreanism under Apollonius of Tyana and Alexander of Abonuteichos do involve, at least in the latter case, the establishment of a cult that was vigorously opposed by Epicureans and Christians, the records leave no examples of defection in either direction.[2]

Heinrich von Staden describes a rift in the medical school (*hairesis*) of Herophilus, an Alexandrian physician (third century BCE) famous for his anatomical discoveries and use of dissection. One of his pupils, Philinus, "turned renegade and founded a rival Alexandrian school with a radically different methodological and epistemological orientation: the Empiricist *hairesis*."[3] In view of the strong sense of inherited tradition of the Herophilean school and its associated cult, paralleled in the establishment of an offshoot with the same features at Laodicea in Asia Minor in the first century BCE, and the fact that Philinus rejected the very innovations for which Herophilus was renowned, Philinus could be considered a defector. Medical, like philosophical, schools were called *haireseis* (in the neutral sense) and had a strong sense of identity, so that abandoning one of them and its

1. Sedley (1989:102). His evidence is both ancient (Cicero, *Nat. d.* 1.10) and modern (Karl Popper).

2. Burkert (1982:18–22).

3. Von Staden (1982:78).

distinctive principles and starting another was perhaps akin to defection in the Jewish and Christian sense.

A somewhat different situation is suggested by a fascinating inscription from Sardis, dated to the first or early second century CE.[4] It instructs the temple-warden devotees in a cult of Zeus the Legislator to desist from participation in the mysteries of Sabazios, Agdistis and Ma:

> In the thirty-nine years of Artaxerxes' reign, Droaphernes son of Barakis, governor of Lydia, dedicated a statue to Zeus the Legislator. He [Droaphernes] instructs his [Zeus's] temple-warden devotees, who enter the innermost sanctum and who serve and crown the god, not to participate in the mysteries of Sabazios with those who bring the burnt offerings and [the mysteries] of Agdistis and Ma. They instruct Dorates the temple-warden to keep away from these mysteries. (CCCA 1.456, trans. Horsley 1981:21–23, no. 3)

The text is apparently a Greek rewriting of an earlier (Aramaic?) edict (ca. 365 BCE) relating to the cult of Zeus Baradates ("Legislator")—a Greek translation of the name of a Persian deity (Ahura Mazda)—suggesting an originally Iranian association that had taken on a Greek form. The prohibition is updated to bring into line one Dorates, who has transgressed it, though precisely who is laying down the law remains obscure. While the edict seems to apply only to the functionaries of the cult and not to the general membership, it nevertheless provides a fascinating glimpse of a religious exclusivism and conservatism that flies in the face of the notion of relaxed and casual religious syncretism in the pagan world. It is at most an example of temporary defection (unless Dorates defied the edict), but it does alert us to the issue of rivalry among groups within paganism.

A quite different example, only briefly related in our sources, is the shift of allegiance attributed to Flavius Clemens and his wife Domitilla. They were accused of "atheism" and "drifting into Jewish ways" (Dio

---

4. Richard Ascough's paper "Religion in Sardis and Smyrna: Survey Papers, Greco-Roman Religions," presented to the Canadian Society of Biblical Studies in 1998, drew this to my attention. See also the discussion in Horsley (1981:21–23); Harland (2003:183).

Cassius 67.14.1–3), and as a result, Clemens was executed and his wife exiled. Some have argued that the two had drifted toward Christianity rather than Judaism, which is a possible understanding of the accusations, since Christians were accused of atheism and could broadly be said to have adopted Jewish ways. Eusebius later refers to a Domitilla who was the niece of Flavius Clemens and who was exiled under Domitian "as a testimony to Christ" (*Hist. eccl.* 3.18.4). If the two Domitillas are conflated, then she was a Christian, but there is no good reason to do so and no evidence that Flavius Clemens was moving toward Christianity rather than Judaism.

Thus we may have the following: Flavius Clemens and his wife moving from paganism toward Judaism, and their niece moving from paganism (or Judaism?) toward Christianity. In each case, we are dealing with Roman aristocrats whose defection would have been seen as a serious matter at the best of times, but since Flavius Clemens and his wife were also the parents of Domitian's designated heirs, political concerns would have been paramount. Perhaps this, rather than their religious predilections, was the real problem, and some have suggested that the charge of judaizing was merely a pretext in a dynastic and political struggle. Yet it remains interesting that defection from paganism—to Judaism or to Christianity—could plausibly be used as a charge and could provoke such a severe reaction from the emperor.

These scraps of evidence suggest that the concept of defection was not unknown in connection with religious cults or *collegia*. Indeed, some of the best evidence arises in connection with an allied phenomenon, the philosophical schools. For example, Dio Chrysostom was a figure associated with shifting allegiance in the philosophical world. It has been common to see him as a "convert" from Sophism to philosophy (to Cynicism at first and then, after his exile, to Stoicism). A man of substance and influence, he had turned his rhetorical skills against the philosophers when they were under attack in the time of Vespasian and Domitian. But then his world fell apart and he too was exiled, an experience that led him to reflect deeply on the profound issues of human existence, drawing on the very philosophies he had once despised (Nock 1933:173–74). But this is now seen as a misleading and simplified view of his career. The notion of a "conversion" is muddied by the fact that he was trained as a Stoic (under Musonius) and may deliberately have obscured his philosophical allegiance and concocted the notion of a conversion to cover up his earlier time-serving attacks on the philosophers (Moles 1978). Even so, it seems likely that there is some truth to stories of his increased attraction to asceticism and profound (if eclectic) philosophical reflection in later life.

In a general way, Dio Chrysostom can be considered an example of changing allegiance, but there are far more pointed examples associated with the various philosophical schools, and it is worth returning to the evidence for this that I hinted at in chapter 1. For example, Dionysus of Heraclea is named in some sources as "the renegade":

> Dionysus, the Renegade *(ho Metathemenos),* declared that pleasure was the end of action; this under the trying circumstance of an attack of ophthalmia. For so violent was his suffering that he could not bring himself to call pain a thing indifferent. . . . At the outset of his career he was fond of literature and tried his hand at all kinds of poetry; afterwards he took Aratus for his model, whom he tried to imitate. When he fell away from Zeno *(apostas de tou Zenonos),* he went over to the Cyreniacs, and used to frequent houses of ill fame and indulge in all other excesses without disguise. After living till he was nearly eighty years of age, he committed suicide by starving himself. (Diog. L. 7.166–67, trans. Hicks 1925)

Originally the pupil of Heraclides, Dionysus eventually became a follower of Zeno the Stoic, whom he then abandoned. The story goes that he defected because his own experience of pain (ophthalmia in Diogenes Laertius, kidney stones in Cicero, *Tusc.* 2.25.60–61) proved to him that his long-held belief that pain was a matter of indifference was false. As a consequence, he allied himself with the hedonist Cyreniacs. This looks very much like an instance of defection provoked by experience contradicting belief.

Timocrates, like his brother Metrodorus a dedicated Epicurean, abandoned the Epicurean school and became its implacable opponent.

> Again there was Timocrates, the brother of Metrodorus, who was his disciple and then left the school. He in the book entitled *Merriment* asserts that Epicurus vomited twice a day from over-indulgence, and

goes on to say that he himself had much ado to escape from those notorious midnight philosophizings and confraternity with all its secrets; further, that Epicurus's acquaintance with philosophy was small and his acquaintance with life even smaller; that his bodily health was pitiful, so much so that for many years he was unable to rise from his chair; and that he spent a whole *mina* daily on his table, as he himself says in his letter to Leontion and in that to the philosophers at Mitylene. He alleges too that in his thirty-seven books *On Nature* Epicurus uses much repetition and writes largely in sheer opposition to others. . . . Epicurus used to call this Nausiphanes jellyfish, an illiterate, a fraud, and a trollop; Plato's school he called "the toadies of Dionysius," their master himself the "golden" Plato, and Aristotle a profligate, who after devouring his patrimony took to soldiering and selling drugs; Protagoras a pack-carrier and the scribe of Democritus and village school-teacher; Heraclitus a muddler; Democritus Lerocritus (the nonsense-monger); and Antidorus Sannidorus (fawning gift-bearer); the Cynics enemies of Greece; the Dialecticians despoilers; and Pyrrho an ignorant boor. (Diog. L. 10.6–8, trans. Hicks 1925)

Both Metrodorus and Epicurus wrote refutations of Timocrates' polemical attacks on their school, but Timocrates still became an influential source for the anti-Epicurean tradition. Among the reasons for this split, Diogenes Laertius lists the following: Epicurus was a glutton and in poor health; he had only limited knowledge of philosophy and real life; he encouraged courtesans to join their school; he had few original thoughts; and he expended most of his energy on dismissive and satirical criticisms of his philosophical predecessors and contemporaries.[5] Many others laid similar charges, but they often seem to echo Timocrates who, unlike most of them, was for a while one of the inner circle of disciples.

It is hard to get beyond the polemical slant of Timocrates' exposé. Some Epicurean positions were easy to distort—such as their qualified hedonism or their encouragement of philosophical training for

5. Sedley (1976) argues in detail for Timocrates as the source of much of the anti-Epicurean tradition.

women—and Timocrates, like his anti-Epicurean successors, took full advantage of this. In general his criticisms concern two things: communal lifestyle and intellectual pretension. The first created a sort of claustrophobia and the second disillusionment with the lack of original thought. Such things may have rankled and may genuinely have precipitated his defection, but a lot of it looks like post facto justification and polemics too. It is not unusual for certain types of defector—those who become active opponents of the group they have abandoned—to exaggerate the shortcomings of the community they have left and give to everything a negative twist. It would also not be unknown for them to attribute their defection to grand motives when the reality may have been more mundane: a perceived slight, a dispute over one of the courtesans, frustrated ambition, or, in the case of Timocrates, a tiff with his brother.[6]

In refutation of Timocrates, Diogenes Laertius notes the widespread respect for Epicurus and the long-term success of his school; he also points out that only one other defector was known. Metrodorus of Stratonica—who lived in the second century BCE and is not the same person as Timocrates' brother—left the Epicureans and "went over to Carneades [i.e., the Academy]" (*pros Karneaden apochoresantos*, Diog. L. 10.9–11). The obscure reason given by Diogenes Laertius that he was "perhaps burdened by his master's excessive goodness" seems to imply that the community ideals (perhaps their austerity?) were too demanding. Something similar may have driven Timocrates out, though that is certainly not the story he told.

Epicureans were far more communally minded than other philosophical schools. They lived together in well-ordered communities that resembled miniature states. Their routine also included quasi-religious elements, such as commemorative festivals, common meals, ceremonies honoring the founder (the "sole savior" Epicurus), and the extensive display of statues of the founders.[7] So defecting from them

6. Sedley suggests that a fratricidal split was at the root of things (1976:153n34). He also thinks Timocrates may have joined the Academy. See also Frischer (1982:50–52).

7. Glad (1995:8–9); Frischer (1982:52–70); Clay (1998) notes the broad similarities between Epicureans and Christians to outsiders, something observed as early as the second century CE (Lucian). "Both groups were charged with atheism, separateness and

would have been more dramatic and obvious than defection from many other philosophical schools. When it involved one of the original inner circle who then turned savagely against his former teachers and colleagues, the seriousness of the defection was compounded.

A famous schism occurred in the Platonic Academy under Antiochus of Ascalon (died 68 BCE).[8] He introduced a reform that created a "new" Academy, but one that they preferred to call the "Old Academy" because they claimed to be harking back to the original teachings of Platonism. Cicero implies that Antiochus's change was sudden and radical, a sort of conversion (*Luc.* 63, 69), after which he became an eclectic philosopher. Ancient writers hint at a number of causes—the desire to have his own following, or his increasing inability to defend the philosophy of the Academy (Cicero, *Luc.* 70)—but nothing certain is known. It seems likely that his intellectual conversion came first and his institutional defection from the Academy some time later. He was thus for all intents and purposes a defector from Scepticism, and some of his followers, like Cicero, were seen in the same light (Cicero, *Luc.* 5; *Acad.* 1.12.43). Equally interesting are the two figures Aristo of Alexandria and Cratippus of Pergamum, both of whom were said to have "defected from the Academy" *(apostatesantes tes Akademeias)* when Aristus, Antiochus's brother, took over the reins.[9]

There are a number of other allusions to schisms in the philosophical schools, but they are sparse in details. Menedemus, failing to become the head of the Academic School, founded another school, but not necessarily in another tradition (*Ind. Acad.* col. 6). Stilpo of Megara in Greece, a talented and evidently persuasive philosopher, attracted a large following from those who originally allied themselves with his philosophical competitors. Even some who set out to refute him became devoted adherents (Diog. L. 2.113–14). Those who joined him

---

secrecy, misanthropy, social irresponsibility, the disruption of families, sexual immorality and general moral depravity" (Glad 1995:9n16). See also Ascough (1998:41–46).

8. Barnes (1989) is the fullest study of Antiochus known to me. I merely summarize some of his observations.

9. The quotation is from the *Index Academicorum* col. 35 (not available to me), quoted in Cancik (1997:691). The examples in the next section are discussed by Cancik on pp. 686–95.

were in a broad sense "converts," and thus from another point of view, defectors. But it is not said that either they or the teachers/schools they left saw it this way. Bion of Borysthenes shifted allegiance several times and was successively a follower of the Academy, the Cynics, the Theodorean atheists, and finally the Peripatetics. He is described as something of a gadfly, easily influenced but also a talented parodist who loved public recognition. For all his bravado and wit, and a lifetime of ridiculing religion, he supposedly turned to the gods and repented of his irreligion in his dying moments (Diog. L. 4.51–58). One could think of him as a serial defector, constitutionally incapable of staying any one course for long. Finally, we may note that Lucian speaks of abandoning *(apostantas)* philosophy and living an ordinary life because of the difficulty of making a choice *(hairesis)* between the various systems of thought *(Hermot.* 67.7).[10] If Bion's problem was his susceptibility to the attractions of the different schools, Lucian's was the uncertainty and confusion caused by their competing claims.

The most striking thing about the evidence for pagan defections is that a great deal of it relates to the philosophical schools rather than to the other sorts of voluntary association *(collegia/thiasoi)* known to us. Cancik has argued that this is precisely the place to look for an analogy to the institutional history, including rifts and defections, of Christianity (and, we might add, Judaism). For it is here, and not in the history of Greco-Roman religions, that we find a concern with unity, inheritance and continuity.[11] There is clearly some truth in this, at least as far as our evidence goes. It is commonly observed that "philosophy" is the nearest thing in the ancient world to our term *religion,* and we know that Christian (like Jewish) apologists often presented themselves as a sort of philosophy.[12] In the second century CE, the analogy came naturally to Galen, who likened Judaism and Christianity to the medical and philosophical schools of his day. It is not implausible to think that on a social

10. This is, of course, not the same as the conflation of the notions of apostasy and heresy we looked at in chapter 1.

11. Cancik suggests that divisions and defections were more common in the philosophical schools than our sources let on (1997:693–95). His main purpose is to find an analogy to the institutional history depicted in Acts.

12. See Wilken (1971); Alexander (1994); Ascough (1998:29–49); and, above all, on Jewish and Christian evidence, Mason (1996).

level, and perhaps on a linguistic level too, the philosophical schools may well have influenced the way that early Christians conceived of and responded to dissidence and defection. Some philosophical schools would have provided a better analogy than others—the Epicureans, for example, who shared an emphasis on tradition and transmission and who were more communally and religiously minded than other schools.

The question we might then consider is whether "philosophy" is a collective concept akin to Judaism or Christianity, so that the school divisions are akin to internal fissions in those communities, or whether defecting from one school to another was akin to moving from, say, Judaism or paganism to Christianity. There is also no doubt that some associations with a strong devotional component, such as the mystery cults, did not demand exclusive commitment from their members. Thus, in the famous case of Apuleius, it was possible to boast of notching up initiations into the various mysteries as if it were a mark of peculiar devotion (Apuleius, *Apol.* 55). This might seem to exclude the notion of defection in principle. Yet I suspect, though I cannot yet confirm, that it was not so simple and that Apuleius and his ilk were an exception. It is probable that most people were in effect committed to one association—with its own rules, traditions, and forms of devotion—in a way that would have distinguished them from adherents to other associations. If such devotees were to leave, as I assume some of them did, because of disaffection or a host of other reasons unknown to us, I suspect they would have been in their own minds, and in those of their former friends, defectors. In this broad sense, all Gentile converts to Christianity or Judaism could be seen as defectors from paganism. The problem that Christians, in particular, had with Roman officials who took a dim view of their attachment to this new superstition, in part because of the way that it interfered with their devotion to civic and imperial cults, points in the same direction.

5

CONCLUSION

J. G. Barclay on Jewish Apostasy

When I first took an interest in the phenomenon of apostasy, there was very little written on it, and most of what there was consisted of brief and unsophisticated accounts based on incomplete inventories of the evidence. Since then—at least in connection with Judaism—there has been a significant change, one that is almost entirely due to the work of John Barclay. I briefly noted his work in the opening chapter, but it deserves greater attention. His attempt to create a taxonomy of the different degrees to which diaspora Jews were affected by Hellenistic culture, a taxonomy that at one extreme includes those who could be considered to have effectively abandoned the Jewish community, is by far the most sophisticated and subtle account of the issue currently available. One of the Jews he pays particular attention to is Paul, the classic early Christian candidate for inclusion in any list of Jewish apostates, and he draws on his larger study of diaspora Judaism for this case. He uses the sociological literature on acculturation to help construct a complex grid that could include the wide range of individual examples (Barclay 1995b; 1996:82–102). In the process, he develops three categories—assimilation, acculturation and accommodation—each of which provides a scale for measuring different kinds and different degrees of adaptation to the outside world. It is worth briefly summarizing his results.

Assimilation defines the degree of social integration with surrounding society. At one extreme were those Jews who consciously shunned contact with the outside world; at the other extreme were those who had abandoned their distinctive customs and practices and fully assimilated to non-Jewish ways. In reality the extremes were rare and most stood somewhere in between. Note, too, that many degrees of assimilation were possible before the point of defection was reached.[1]

Figure 1 *Assimilation (Social Integration)*

Abandonment of key
Jewish social distinctives
|
Gymnasium education
|
Attendance at Greek athletics/theater
|
Commercial employment
with non-Jews
|
Social life confined to the
Jewish community

Acculturation refers to adaptation to the nonmaterial, especially educational aspects of the surrounding culture, in particular exposure to and a knowledge of its language and literary heritage, its philosophies and its cardinal virtues.

1. The diagrams below are from Barclay (1996:93–97).

Figure 2 *Acculturation (Language/Education)*

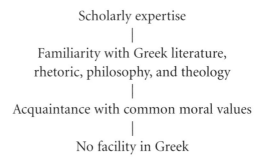

Scholarly expertise
|
Familiarity with Greek literature,
rhetoric, philosophy, and theology
|
Acquaintance with common moral values
|
No facility in Greek

Accommodation defines the extent to which knowledge of the surrounding culture is employed—for example, by accommodating Greek ideas (as with Philo) or by opposing them (as in 3 Maccabees). At one end there is an urge to absorb and integrate and at the other to oppose and eschew it.

Figure 3 *Accommodation (Use of Acculturation)*

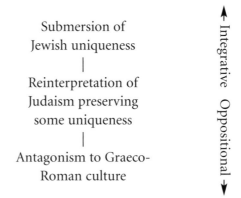

Submersion of
Jewish uniqueness
|
Reinterpretation of
Judaism preserving
some uniqueness
|
Antagonism to Graeco-
Roman culture

Integrative Oppositional

Using these different scales, Barclay considers a number of examples, of which the following are of particular interest to us:

- 4 Maccabees reveals a reasonably high level of acculturation (the author knows Greek and Greek rhetoric, etc.), a minimal degree of accommodation ("philosophy" is narrowly identified with "instruction in the law") and virtually no desire for assimilation (it is designed to counter assimilationist tendencies).

- Philo's allegorizers/assimilators, whose activities were discussed above (see *Migr.* 89–93; *Mos.* 1.31; *Conf.* 2–13), show a high degree of acculturation (they are familiar with Greek thought and Greek hermeneutical procedures), accommodation (they place a high value on Greek culture), and assimilation (they have abandoned Jewish customs and identity markers).
- Paul, who is moderately acculturated (he uses Greek language and rhetoric but knows Pharisaic/Jewish forms of argument too), generally resists accommodation (he condemns Jewish and Greek wisdom alike) but, in his Christian stage, is strongly assimilated (he is willing to "live like a Gentile" if only for tactical reasons).

Earlier discussions of apostasy, such as they were, dealt in simpler categories that were less sensitive to the realities of life for Jews in the Hellenistic world. The usefulness of Barclay's analysis is his inclusion of both different kinds and different degrees of adaptation, creating a grid that better reflects the complex world of antiquity. It shows, for example, that the use of Greek, while in some ways a sign of outside influence, can coexist with a passionate refusal to conform to, or even place any value on, Greek culture. It also shows that there were many ways of existing between the extremes of assimilation and apostasy, a view that an important recent work has reinforced (Gruen 2002). Indeed, it is likely that this is precisely where the majority of diaspora (and Palestinian) Jews found themselves, a space where what was and what was not acceptable was a matter of constant and changing debate.

With Jews, Barclay notes, the key indicator of apostasy is assimilation. The issue then becomes one of drawing the line, and the questions become where is it to be drawn and who is to draw it? There is, he says, no absolute answer and no objective standard by which Jews (or others) can be assessed. We cannot, in the end, say who were apostates, only who those in the ancient world thought were apostates. For this reason, Barclay thinks that Paul is properly seen as an apostate because his behavior (assimilation) led other Jews of his time to label him so. There is an important truth here, and we do well to remember it, but it is an extreme position that one senses even Barclay is not altogether happy with. For one thing, the judgment of others is not the only aspect to think about. Some think that Paul consciously defected from Judaism, as we discovered above. That is, he knew exactly what he was doing and could scarcely have been oblivious of the way in which his newfound faith overturned the old. For another, we have to bear in mind that in internecine struggles—among Christians, for example— the label of apostate/defector could be bandied around loosely and used of people whom we might properly consider to be just another variant of the Christian movement.

As a way of assessing the evidence for apostasy, Barclay's scheme works best for Jews and Jewish Christians, and it was of course designed with those groups in mind—that is, minority groups with distinctive customs which are required to react in one way or another to a larger outside world. Barclay's model is less useful if we try to adapt it to most Christian and pagan evidence—though I should add that this was not his intention. For example, Gentile Christians faced the reverse problem. They were already part of the majority pagan culture, and their challenge was to assess how much of this they needed to shed to conform to the mores of the cultural subgroup that they had joined. Prior to their conversion, the influence of pagan culture would have been all-pervasive, though the level at which this operated would have varied according to the extent of their education. In the early decades, many of them would have been married to non-Christians; depending on their position in the household, such marriages could have profound effects on their continuing exposure to the mores of the cultural majority (see below). Some Christians, like some Jews, resisted accommodation or assimilation, but the dynamic was not the same. One group gave something up, the other took it on board. For Gentile Christians, apostasy typically meant drifting back to a world and a lifestyle they had formerly known; for Jews it meant experiencing them for the first time. The situation facing the Jews perhaps finds a closer analogy among second-generation Christians and their successors, when households began to be nurtured in a distinctively Christian environment with peculiar practices, mores, and beliefs that separated them from the world outside. The number of adherents who came through this route rather than directly from a pagan environment is, however, not known. To complicate matters a little further, we should also note that some Christian defectors assimilated not (back) to paganism but to Judaism. That is, there were now three rather than two players on the stage. Finally, we note that for many of our pagan examples, the acculturation/assimilation scheme is not relevant, since their defection is not defined in these terms at all.

Even if we were to agree in principle that there is no absolute and final way of marking where assimilation becomes defection, because in the end everything depends on the arbitrary judgment of others, there are examples so egregious that they invite us to make some important distinctions. We may still ask who from among those we have surveyed might be considered extreme assimilationists and thus candidates for the label "apostate." By "extreme" I mean those who abandoned in a significant way the central or distinctive beliefs and practices that defined their group. In the first instance, we depend on the judgment of their contemporaries, but we are not bound by them. We can make our own judgments—arbitrary perhaps, but not without some basis. We have not accepted, for example, some of the internecine Christian struggles as examples of apostasy even though such language was used at the time. Nor would we accept the perspective of some ancient (and modern) writers that assimilation was tantamount to apostasy, so that receiving a Greek education, attending the theater and games (as did Philo), or even seeking Greek citizenship inexorably defined one as an apostate (cf. 3 Maccabees).

Since the notions of acculturation/assimilation are usually applied in the context of normal, everyday life, we should probably in this context also put to one side all those who were forced to defect by the pressures of war or persecution. True, the crises that precipitated these defections may have arisen in the context of ongoing pressures to assimilate, but they also introduced exceptional conditions that muddy the picture. Of the remaining examples, the following seem to be those whose assimilationist instincts took them beyond the generally recognized boundaries of their community and qualify them for the label "defector": Antiochus of Antioch; those represented by Zambri in Josephus; Elisha ben Abuyah; Paul; Tiberius Alexander; the proselyte defectors in Josephus; various groups in Philo; Jews in Suetonius; Christians in Pliny; Christians in *Hermas*. As a special category, we might also mention those Gentile Christians who appeared to have defected not by reverting to the dominant surrounding culture, but by turning to Judaism (Revelation, *Barnabas,* Justin).

In another essay, Barclay (1995a) has developed a somewhat different way of understanding apostasy using the sociology of deviance, especially from the "interactionist" or "societal reaction" perspective. This approach does concern itself with the setting of boundaries, norms, and laws—and that is of some interest to our overall assessment of defection—but its main concern is with the social production of deviance and with labeling. Social production emphasizes the view that deviance is defined not by the quality of particular acts or attitudes in themselves but by the negative social reaction they evoke. Society defines what is deviant, and it may, and often does, apply its own standards selectively. The important thing is not so much that acts and attitudes are displayed (though they have to be present) but that they are reacted to as deviant by society. Labeling is the consequence of society's reaction, when society has successfully defined someone or something as deviant. This can in turn have further effects, since in some instances the label encourages people or groups to adopt a deviant career, to act out the label that has been applied to them.

In principle this approach "does not provide an 'aetiology' of deviant acts, neither does the interactionist perspective in itself explain why societies react as they do to acts they consider 'deviant.'"[2] In reality a number of theorists do interest themselves in theories of power or social control, and those who suggest that the labeling of deviants has an important role in boundary maintenance among insecure or minority communities have caught the eye of those interested in early Christianity and Judaism. In essence this approach to social behavior provides us with "an angle of enquiry, rather than a 'theory' or 'model' generating predictive hypotheses" (Barclay 1995a:118). It provides a perspective and suggests interesting questions.

One of Barclay's motives in using this approach is to insist, as do the interactionist theorists, that apostasy, like deviance, is not an

---

2. Barclay (1995a:117). This summary of deviance theory is taken from his article. Jack T. Sanders also has a useful summary of deviance theory, but his interest is in applying it to the Jewish-Christian schism as a whole rather than to individuals (1993:129–51).

objectively definable entity. It is rather a matter of perspective. This brings Barclay back to one of the issues he considered elsewhere: the relationship between labeling and reality, and in particular the power of the former to create the latter. Put more pointedly: do apostates exist only because their contemporaries so label them, and is that all there is to be said? Barclay rightly notes that among Jews an apostate could be defined differently from one writer to another, from one time to another, and from one set of circumstances to another. But he qualifies this relativistic conclusion too when he suggests that idolatrous worship or the eating of unclean food were things about which there was a fair degree of unanimity in Jewish communities of the period (1995a:119). Jews who transgressed these taboos were likely to be considered defectors by virtually all other Jews of whatever stripe.

What do we gain from this approach? First, we are invited to ask who a person labels as a defector/apostate and, if possible, why. In most of our examples, the perspective is that of the labeler, not the labeled. Whether the labeled would have accepted the label, or whether they would have had a different explanation of their behavior and its effects, can rarely be seen. It is probable at any rate that "apostate" was a label that people did not often or publicly attach to themselves—an assumption confirmed by some modern research, which suggests that apostates, even when they recognize their position (which, in some of the examples we have considered, they may not have), tend not to advertise their defection (Bromley 1988:25; Barker 1985:178–79).

Second, one qualification of this relativistic perspective is, I think, important, and has been touched on already. Most of the cases of defection we have found reveal attitudes and behavior that were an affront to the central convictions and norms of the group the defectors had abandoned, and these norms and convictions were sufficiently widespread in the respective communities that we can, I think, consider the labeling to have a certain objective quality—allowing that we agree that defectors are reasonably defined as those who abandon the central or distinctive beliefs and practices of their community.

Third, I keep mentioning beliefs and attitudes as well as behavior. The sociology of deviation looks mostly at behavior, partly because it is observable in a way that attitudes are not. Interestingly, when we look at our list of defectors, in almost every case, the thing that evokes the judgment that they are defectors is their behavior rather than their beliefs. The familiar contrast between the Christian emphasis on belief and the Jewish emphasis on praxis is not confirmed by this evidence.

The Sociology of Apostasy

In the last two decades, sociologists have taken a renewed interest in the phenomenon of apostasy in the modern world. It has become something of a refrain among them that, compared with the long-established interest in conversion, the problem of apostasy (otherwise described as defection, disaffiliation, disengagement, disidentification, dropping out, leave-taking) has been neglected. Most studies note that defection can be gradual or dramatic, casual or (more commonly) traumatic. It is also noted that people may be disaffected with or mentally withdrawn from their group before actually leaving it. Apostasy in this context can cover anything from the gradual, barely noticeable drifting away from a long-established membership in a religious community to the more dramatic extraction and deprogramming of converts from religious cults. The evidence that is tapped can be as broad as census data, as focused as the intensive study of particular religious groups, or as personal as the autobiographical accounts of those leaving a religious order. Some of this, while interesting in itself, is of limited use in considering the ancient evidence because it is profoundly defined by the circumstances and values of the modern world.[3] The sort of difficulty we have in passing from the modern to the ancient world is illustrated in Hadaway (1989), where the typology of apostates includes Successful Swinging Singles, Sidetracked Singles, Young Settled Liberals, Young Libertarians, and Irreligious Traditionalists. Similarly, in twentieth-century America— often the field where such data have been collected—forced apostasy under the threat of death, which was common in the ancient world, is not mentioned.

3. Bromley (1988) has the most useful collection of essays. A useful recent discussion of modern Jewish defectors is found in Endelman (1987).

Thus the evidence of modern sociological studies has to be used selectively and handled with care. In the lead essay of a collection, David Bromley (1998a), a prominent figure in the sociological discussion of apostasy, makes a series of distinctions that attempt to clarify the labels and categories used to describe the phenomenon in the modern world. He distinguishes three sorts of organizations, understood as ideal types, that actual organizations approximate to varying degrees. Allegiant organizations are those that have a high degree of social legitimacy (e.g., mainstream churches, medical organizations) and that have sufficient standing to be allowed to resolve disputes internally. Contestant organizations (e.g., profit-making economic organizations) have a degree of acceptance but are also subject to challenge and constraint especially from regulatory agencies. Subversive organizations (e.g., alternative religious movements, radical political groups) are those least in tune with mainstream society, by which they are considered threatening or illegitimate. They are afforded almost no organizational legitimacy and are subjected to coercion and control by those who think they subvert the social order. These ideal types are defined, therefore, primarily in terms of their degree of tension with society at large.

Bromley then uses these three organizational types to define three different categories of "exiters" or "leavetakers." *Defectors* are those who leave allegiant organizations whose authorities control the exit process and facilitate role transition (e.g., priests and nuns leaving Catholic orders). *Whistleblowers* are those who appeal to external authorities in their attempt to challenge and expose the corruption of organizational practices, and who may not initially have any intention of leaving the organization itself. *Apostates* Bromley restricts in this context to those who exit a movement in a highly polarized situation, declaring a total change of loyalty without the consent or control of the organization and typically allying themselves with its opponents (e.g., those who leave cults or new religious movements (NRMs). In making these distinctions, Bromley deliberately gives these terms quite specific meanings: "Apostate refers not to ordinary religious leavetakers (the general referent) but to that subset of leavetakers who are involved in contested exit and who affiliate with an oppositional coalition" (1998a:5). This is in line with the sociological rather than the theological use of the term *apostate,* where the latter refers generally to the renouncing of one's religion (Shupe 1998:209–11).[4]

In this scheme, the category of whistleblower, as Bromley admits, is rarely relevant to religious organizations in the United States because they are not usually subject to regulatory control by the state, and the category is of little value in terms of the ancient evidence as well. While *defector* and *apostate* are used loosely, indeed often synonymously, Bromley's attempt to formulate a clear distinction is not without merit. In terms of the ancient evidence, the distinction itself, or at least a modified form of it, is more interesting than the three organizational types he bases it on. In adapting his idea, we could use *defector* for those who exit with relatively little fuss—because they drift away gradually, prevaricate, retain some affection for the organization, or because the organization is grateful to see the back of them, among many other motives we could imagine—and *apostate* for those whose leave-taking is decisive, radical, and often results in public hostility on both sides. An apostate is thus an extreme version of a defector, the defector who turns into an enemy of the organization left behind. Apostates go out with a bang, defectors with a whimper.

A couple of other essays in this volume have some relevance to our theme. Eileen Barker (1998:75–93) usefully notes the existence of peripheral or marginal members of NRMs. Indeed, she distinguishes them. Peripheral members are those who were core members but who have loosened their ties without giving up their association altogether. They, and the organization, have adapted to their living on the edge. Marginal members, by contrast, are those who see themselves and are seen by others to be core members but who dispute some central belief or practice of the organization. This sort of distinction, useful in well-documented modern examples, cannot meaningfully be made in the more sparsely attested ancient examples. Nevertheless, we do find the phenomenon of marginality in the broader sense, and Barker's distinction reminds us that disaffection and defection can be expressed in many different ways.

---

4. In the same volume, Carter, on the other hand, wants to retain the "less specifically role-related sense of one who has (or appears to have) abandoned a belief, faith or cause" (1998:226).

Daniel Johnson (1998:115–37) analyzes the fascinating phenomenon of fictional or semi-fictional apostate narratives, when there is credible evidence that "the avowed apostate was not who he or she claims to have been 'back then,' and thus is not the authoritative voice he or she claims to be now." These are "the apostates who never were" (1998:116). While I can think of no specific ancient example to which this applies, it does raise interesting questions about the understanding of apostasy as a definition or label imposed from the outside that we examined in relation to Barclay's discussion of Jewish apostates. Clearly, in the modern world there are examples of individuals who openly claim to be defectors or apostates; indeed, in some cases discussed by Johnson, they make a career out of it. While the claims of some are questionable, that is not true of all, and in either case, it is the autobiographical claim itself that is interesting, suggesting that self-labeling has to be added to the concept of labeling by others.

Used with due caution, sociological studies of apostasy can thus be helpful as we try to think about analogous cases in the ancient world. Another example of the way they might help is in their focus on the motives for and causes of defection, something for which there is good evidence in the modern world and almost none from the ancient world. But the lack in one can be partly made up by the surfeit in the other, as long as we do not jump uncritically from the one to the other. In one of the more interesting recent studies, Stuart Wright (1987) surveyed ninety people involved with three different NRMs, in each case including fifteen who left and fifteen who stayed.[5] His concern was with voluntary defectors, and he claims that defection from NRMs can be seen as "a type of desocialization process whereby one loses identification with a social group(s). It involves the transformation of identity, social relations, and worldview." Defection, he notes, is a process, but certain experiences and events are fundamentally more important in creating dissonance and engendering defection. He isolates five factors that would appear to contribute the most:

---

5. The quotation in the next sentence is from Wright (1987:7). Like others, he likens the process of defection to that of divorce.

- Social insulation: the more contacts with the outside world, the greater the incidence of defection.
- Dyadic relations: the less regulated they are, especially in the case of marital relations, the greater the chance of defection.
- Urgency: a sense of imminence or urgency (as in the belief that the end is near) creates a reason for sacrifice and binds people to the group; the less that exists, the more likely it is that defection will occur.
- Affective needs: the less the community provides for affective needs, as a surrogate family or society, the more people are likely to defect.
- Leadership: the behavioral inconsistencies of leaders lead to disillusionment and defection.

Most of these factors were confirmed in Wright's survey, except the fourth, since many defectors claimed that the best part of membership was their relationship with other members (not the leaders). He notes other contributing factors too: the attraction of alternatives, though this kicked in mainly after the initial defection; and the fact that for many young people (a high percentage of NRM members) commitment was short but intense, a form of social experimentation that eventually succumbed to the pull of close family ties. Modes of exit he categorizes as follows: *covert*—those (usually long-standing members) with vague discontents and strong outside relationships; *overt*—those with a stronger reaction to specific policies or beliefs; and *declarative*—those who make their exit confrontational.

I have summarized Wright's work to give the flavor of this type of study. His conclusions are confirmed and expanded by others. Some of the more interesting results from the studies that I have found most useful for a consideration of defection in the ancient world are:

- The importance of family ties. Some have argued that for young people defection may be a rebellion against parental control (Hoge 1988; Albrecht et al. 1988), though this has been challenged (Hunsberger 1980; 1983); others emphasize the importance of strong family ties in encouraging devotees to abandon an NRM (Brinkerhoff and Mackie 1992; Sherkat and Wilson 1995). This could be included in Wright's more general category of contacts with the outside world. From the ancient world, we might think of the willing Hellenizers of 1 Maccabees, various groups in Josephus and Philo, *Hermas,* and some Christians in Cyprian. A subset is those attracted to a community with which they had previously had contact: Josephus's proselyte defectors, Hebrews, *1 Clement, Barnabas,* and Justin.

- Excessive regulation of lifestyle and the imposition of rigid demands (Hoge 1988; Albrecht et al. 1988; Brinkerhoff and Mackie 1992; Jacobs 1989), with which we may compare Josephus, Philo, *Hermas,* Peregrinus, Timocrates, and Metrodorus.
- Social disaffection, with other members and especially with leaders— the main thesis of another important book on the topic (Jacobs 1989; but see also Mauss 1969; Albrecht et al. 1988; Brinkerhoff and Mackie 1992). This brings to mind Timocrates, Antiochus of Ascalon, and perhaps the Qumran defectors.
- Romance with or marriage to a nonmember (Hoge 1988; Albrecht et al. 1988; Sherkat and Wilson 1995), something we have seen in Josephus, Philo, and Cyprian.
- Intellectual doubt (Mauss 1969; Albrecht et al. 1988; Brinkerhoff and Mackie 1992), for which there is evidence in Tiberius Alexander, Philo's allegorists and antagonists of the law, the Bar Kokhba Christians, Simeon ben Abuyah, Pseudo Cyprian's senator, Ammonius, Julian, and almost all the pagan examples we looked at.
- Upward social mobility (Sherkat and Wilson 1995), as seen also in Tiberius Alexander, Philo's ambitious Jews, Dositheus, *Hermas,* and Cyprian.

Types and Their Motivations

Looking at ancient apostates and defectors through the eyes of their modern equivalents encourages us to try to classify them into broad types. The fit is not perfect, as we would expect given the differences between ancient and modern societies. Yet the work of these sociologists helps us to reflect on and classify some of the examples we have gathered. One way to classify them, for example, is in terms of the process of defection, adapting Wright's categories of covert, overt, and declarative modes of exit.

The first type we might describe as gradual defectors, those who slowly drifted apart from their religious community in order to pursue a life otherwise closed off to them. Their decision was neither precipitate nor a response to an immediate crisis, but was rather a cumulative response to the routine business of defining their position in the world. The circumstances that encouraged them to loosen their ties with their community were quite varied: family ties, intermarriage, social advancement, military or political ambition, or simply a hankering to enjoy the lifestyle of those outside their community. To what degree these factors were the cause or the effect of their gradual disaffiliation cannot be known, but it would be reasonable to suppose that they worked both ways. For many of those involved the process may initially have been imperceptible, a matter of making minor compromises rather than a conscious decision to change allegiance. Yet the cumulative effect of small compromises could eventually lead them to be viewed as apostates by others if not by themselves. Some of the Jews in Alexandria and the Christians in *Hermas* and Cyprian would fit here.

Others we might define as precipitate defectors, those who apparently made a sudden decision to transfer their loyalty elsewhere. Antiochus of Antioch, Paul, Peregrinus, Elisha ben Abuyah, and Antiochus of Ascalon could all be placed in this category, as perhaps could the Jews in Suetonius and the Christians in Pliny. Of course the suddenness of their defection may be deceptive since, as is commonly observed, what looks like a precipitate decision is often the expression of a cumulative process of disillusionment. And when doubts about the beliefs or practices of an organization have been niggling away for some time, the precipitating factor itself may not appear to be particularly dramatic. It can merely be the straw that breaks the camel's back. Unfortunately, in the ancient world, evidence that would allow the reconstruction of this kind of process rarely leaves any trace. Recognition of its plausibility, however, will at least make us cautious about making too clear a distinction between this group and the gradual defectors mentioned above. In both kinds, the process may have been similar, and what may differentiate them is more the style of their leave-taking than the process that led up to it.

A third and related subgroup we might call antagonistic apostates, those who became vigorous and vociferous opponents of the tradition they had left—a phenomenon not unknown in the history of Jewish and Christian apostates down through the ages. Antiochus of Antioch, the "Zambri Jews" of Josephus, some of Philo's intellectually disaffected, Julian the Apostate, and Timocrates come to mind. The rabbinic defector Simeon ben Abuyah may belong here, and some would claim that Paul does too. Those who betrayed their fellow adherents when the heat was on (as in *Hermas* and Cyprian) should probably be included too. For some sociologists, these would, technically speaking, be the only true apostates, since by definition they are distinguished from run-of-the-mill defectors precisely by their active opposition to the organization they have left.

Another, perhaps more interesting, way of classifying defectors is in terms of the cause and the inner motivations for their behavior, the former of which is often more transparent than the latter. A factor that appears in a number of our examples is the pull of social and family networks. Philo speaks of friends and family who entice people to participate in pagan worship, as does Cyprian of those who actively persuade family and friends to accede to Roman pressure. Both Philo and Josephus reflect on the dangers of mixed marriages, and we can certainly suppose that the "atavistic defectors" mentioned below were affected as much by social and family ties as by anything else. Jews, wherever they lived, belonged to communities with notably strong social and family ties and a way of life that was distinctive in the ancient world. This would undoubtedly have exerted a pull on anyone who had drifted away. On the other hand, intimate relations with non-Jews could pull in the other direction. Biblical and postbiblical writings ban intermarriage either with some (Exod 34:15; Deut 7:2-4) or with all (Ezra 9:1-2, 12-14; *Jub.* 30:7-17; 4QMMT 75–82; Philo, *Spec.* 3.29; Josephus, *Ant.* 8.190–96) non-Jews, despite some counterexamples that muddy the issue (Deut 21:10-14, marrying the beautiful female captive). The rabbis also prohibit intermarriage because, in their view, Gentiles are impure.

In all of these attempts to regulate intermarriage, one of the key motives is to protect Jews from sliding into idolatry and apostasy.[6] Yet

---

6. Hayes has a good discussion of the different motives for the ban at various times (1999). A good general survey of Jewish intermarriage is Cohen (1999:241–62).

the incidence of intermarriage in Jewish communities remains uncertain. Prohibitions may be only an attempt to reinforce a norm, a form of preemptive legislation; but they may imply that the issue had not gone away. The Jewish romance *Joseph and Aseneth*, which tells of the conversion and marriage of a Jewish man and a pagan woman, suggests that intermarriage was not unknown, but the marriage is preceded by Aseneth's conversion, which technically makes it a marriage between Jews. Philo and Josephus can be taken to imply, in their rewriting of biblical stories, that intermarriage and its attendant dangers was not an issue that belonged solely to the distant past. The rabbis rarely discuss intermarriage, which may well suggest that they were largely untroubled by it, but among nonrabbinic Jews, things may have been quite different (Cohen 1999:245–48). Clearly, family ties had the potential for encouraging defection as well as for throwing the process into reverse.

If Rodney Stark and others are correct in supposing that social and family networks were the most significant factors in conversions to Christianity, we would expect them to have played an equally significant role in defections too.[7] Even when a household converted, considerable strain would have been put on relations with parents, siblings, and in-laws who did not follow. It would have complicated not only routine social interaction, but questions of education, inheritance, and religious devotion. This is vividly portrayed in the distress of Perpetua's father in the days leading up to her martyrdom (*The Martyrdom of Perpetua and Felicitas*). Her refusal to listen to his pleas is what the Christian writer admires, but his genuine anguish and bafflement shine through too.

Division within a household is most commonly raised in connection with intermarriage, a topic that appears more pointedly in Christian sources, as we would expect from a movement that did most of its recruiting among pagans. At a very early stage, we have Paul's advice that believers married to unbelievers should stay that way unless the unbeliever initiates a separation (1 Cor 7:12-16). The author of 1 Peter urges female Christians to accept the authority of their husbands even if they are pagan (1 Pet 3:1-6). Here and in later sources we

---

7. Stark (1996:3–28). MacMullen also emphasizes the lack of evidence for an active mission after the early decades and the importance of networks in the home, the workplace, and the street corner (1984:33–42).

hear almost exclusively of Christian women married to pagan men and not the reverse, perhaps because the conversion of the paterfamilias would normally involve conversion of the rest of the household too.

Not so with women, even wealthy and influential women. Justin speaks of a new convert who extricates herself with some difficulty from her failing marriage to a dissolute pagan (*1 Apol.* 2), and Tertullian's condemnation of new marriages between Christian women and pagan men indicates that they were a lot more common than he would have liked (*Ux.* 2.3, 8). This could have benefits. Some Christians thought the woman might impress, even convert, her husband by her exemplary life, but successes are rarely reported (MacDonald 2003:157–59). Such Christian women, especially the wealthy and influential, could also persuade their husbands to look favorably on the church.[8] On the other hand, the Christian partner could revert or convert to paganism. From the lack of concern in early Christian sources about losing members through marriage to pagans, Stark concludes that it did not happen (1996:113–15). Perhaps so, but Tertullian's warnings about the danger of contamination through mixed marriages may suggest the opposite. Tertullian was admittedly something of a puritanical extremist, but his view that Christian women were often attracted by the wealth and property of their pagan spouses, if only partially true, would also have meant that they were vulnerable. Nor should we forget that Cyprian mentions marriage with pagans (and love of wealth) as one of the main causes of a church gone slack and made vulnerable to the demand for public defection (*De Lapsis* 6).

Related to the cases mentioned above are the examples of what we might call atavistic defectors, those whose commitment was eventually undercut by the pull of their former lifestyle. The attraction could have been social, cultural, or familial, though in several cases it is not specified. The defecting proselytes mentioned by Josephus seem to have found Judaism too demanding and to have returned to the comfortable world they knew. The Epistle to the Hebrews seems to be addressed to Jewish Christians feeling (and sometimes succumbing to) the pull of

8. Stark argues that exogamous marriages were a significant boost to Christian proselytizing (1996:111–15). MacMullen is doubtful (1984:35), as is MacDonald (2003:157–59), who offers several qualifications.

Judaism, its festivals, its cult, and its deeply rooted connections with the past. The Christians were missing their familiar world, but the author tries hard to convince them that Christianity has more to offer. Justin refers to Jewish Christians who abandoned their belief in Christ and returned to the life of the synagogue, and some think something similar is being alluded to in the reference to "those who say they are Jews but are not" in Revelation. *1 Clement* and *Barnabas* may allude to Jewish or Gentile Christians in the same position, that is, those who have been members of the church but have abandoned it for Judaism. The Christian apostates mentioned in *Hermas* seem to have been heavily motivated by a fear of losing their social and economic standing in Roman society. Their wealth, their business affairs, and their fondness for the pagan lifestyle all pulled them away from the church, especially when they were under the gun. The pressures of persecution could have direct economic and social effects—not just the ultimate penalty, death, but banishment and confiscation of property that brought the whole family tumbling down with the offender. But if in some instances the urge to revert was heightened by external threats, in one case at least *(Barnabas),* it may have been Roman support for the Jews that sparked defections from the Christian community.

The allusions to wealth and social ambition in *Hermas* remind us of the importance of social or political ambition in precipitating defection. If for some it was a case of reluctance to abandon a pre-Christian lifestyle, in at least one place *Hermas* implies that the problem also arose with those who became wealthy after they had joined the Christian movement (*Sim.* 8.9.1–3). The trappings of wealth and influence acquired after conversion led them to drift away. Cyprian, as noted, also mentions the influence of wealth on the decline of the Christian commitment. Social, political, and military advancement were probably also factors in the defection of Tiberius Alexander, as well as of some of the other Alexandrian Jews mentioned by Philo.

There are a few interesting examples of intellectual apostates, those whose disaffection was rooted in serious doubts about the philosophical or theological framework of their Jewish, Christian, or philosophical beliefs. Tiberius Alexander may have had doubts about God's providential rule over the world, and they may have been precipitated or compounded by a Greek education. Other Alexandrian Jews had difficulty with traditional interpretations of scripture. The notorious rabbinic heretic Elisha ben Abuyah *(Aḥer)* may have been driven by his distress at the apparent indifference of God to the fate of his people to move toward a dualistic explanation of the problem of evil in the world. The (probably Jewish) Christians who, according to Justin's account, defected to the synagogue may well have been persuaded to do so by Jews who convinced them of the weakness of Christian claims. Ammonius and, of course, Julian the Apostate were affected by competing intellectual claims, even though other factors may also have played a significant role. Most of the philosophical defectors would fit here too—Dionysus the Renegade, Timocrates, and Antiochus of Ascalon. Both intellectual doubts and objections to a particular lifestyle played their role, as we might expect, in the philosophical schools, where the two often went hand in hand. Doubts about the messianic claims of Bar Kokhba may have precipitated the defection of Jewish Christians from that movement. It was noted above that difficulties with the intellectual claims or lifestyle of a leader have led some to abandon modern cults. Many contemporary Jews and Christians struggle with the issue of theodicy. Most appear to find ways of accommodating it that allow them to remain in their community, but some, faced with horrendous catastrophes such as the Holocaust or with the sheer incoherence of traditional claims, drift away.

Finally, there is the category of forced apostates—those who buckled when severe oppression left them, as often as not, with a choice between defection and death. Quite a few of the examples we have looked at include an element of external force, making it the most frequently documented context for apostasy in the ancient world. The oppressors were usually a foreign power or an unsympathetic state, and even the Bar Kokhba supporters who put pressure on the Jewish Christians can be thought of as a rudimentary government, even if with temporally and geographically limited jurisdiction. It is probable that most of those who defected in such circumstances did so against their will and would not otherwise have considered such a move. Yet for others the situation was more ambiguous. Some Jews in the Maccabean era may have welcomed Hellenization as a progressive move for Judaism; and some Christians in the reign of Trajan, though they may have preferred to stay out of the public eye, were eager to make public their earlier defection when named by informers to the state authorities. It is not implausible to suppose that some Jews and Christians who were forced to apostatize thought that they could remain secret adherents, as has often happened since, and we have two Christian examples that confirm this—Basilides and the *lapsi* in Cyprian. In some cases— as in the Temple Scroll, Antiochus of Antioch and *Hermas*—apostasy was compounded by betrayal of others and evoked the harshest of condemnations. An apostate was one thing, a traitor was another, and for this group there was apparently no way back.

There is little discussion of their modern equivalents in the sociological literature associated with apostasy. Of course, there has been no shortage of oppressive regimes driven by political, religious, or ideological conviction that have oppressed adherents of religious communities—the former Soviet empire and the Balkans, China, and Tibet are only a few of those that immediately come to mind. Some religious devotees succumb to the pressure, some publicly accede but privately cling to their beliefs, and others openly resist and face the consequences.

It is the last of these, the heroic resisters, whom we hear most about in the Western media. Sociologists who study apostasy tend to confine themselves to evidence from the United States—a deeply religious society with an extraordinary array of mainstream religions and minority cults and one in which there has been little conflict between religion and state. Perhaps the closest analogy is to be found in the mass suicide of the Jim Jones cult members in Guyana in 1978 and the Branch Davidians who went down in flames in Waco, Texas, in 1993. They were utopian communities that came into conflict with the established social order, in each case with a violent outcome. Both groups spawned defectors who used their inside knowledge to rouse opposition to them in the media and among political authorities (Hall and Schuyler 1998). From the perspective of the cult members, these defectors were traitors, as no doubt were some Jews and Christians in the early period, though they are usually portrayed in quite the opposite way in society at large.

Of course, these categories are somewhat artificial. They clearly overlap, and other groupings could be devised. Yet they do serve to point us to some of the major motives for defection. Some of them can be readily paralleled in the modern world: gradual drifters, attracted to and then enticed away by aspects of life frowned on within their community; sudden defectors who are seized by an alternative vision; erstwhile converts who cannot resist the pull of their former life; and the intellectually disaffected, gnawed by doubts about traditional beliefs or disturbed by distressing events for which their tradition offers no adequate explanation. Many of these motives for apostasy are honorable, and in some cases, they may speak directly to our own experience. We can at any rate attempt to weigh and understand them with sympathy.

Indelibility and Incidence

Some have argued that in rabbinic literature Jewish apostates retain their status as Jews despite their defection. However egregious their actions, they remain part of Israel. Sometimes this is taken to be the view of the Jewish tradition as a whole. For example, Lawrence Schiffman bases his view on a midrash on Lev 1:2 (Nedabah parasha 2:3), as interpreted in the Babylonian Talmud (*b. Ḥul.* 5a). In the latter passage, the issue concerns who can bring offerings to the Temple: "Whereas all non-Jews (including idolaters) may send voluntary offerings to be sacrificed in the Jerusalem Temple, this right is denied to certain Jews, namely to those who have apostasized [*sic*] to the extent of performing idolatrous worship or violating the sabbath in public. These people are, therefore, still Jews, for if they were excluded from the Jewish people, their offerings would be acceptable" (Schiffman 1985:48–49). S. Stern (1994:109) concurs: "In a sense the apostate is the mirror image of the convert: just as the latter is 'Israel in all respects,' so the apostate is a 'non-Jew in all respects.' However, the apostate differs from the convert in that the latter divests himself entirely from his original non-Jewish identity, whereas the apostate retains his basic identity as Israel, even though it is seldom referred to."[9] Gary Porton argues

9. S. Stern (1994:107–9) refers to Schiffman's evidence, to the phrase *Israel mumar* (i.e., "Israel apostate") in which *Israel* is the substantive and *mumar* the epithet, and to the right of the apostate to marry a Jew (*b. Yev.* 47b).

similarly that even if converts to Judaism subsequently apostatize, they
remain irrevocably part of Israel.[10]

In each case, the point may be technically correct but is substan-
tially insignificant. The evidence is slight, scattered, and obscure. It is
also frequently talmudic, and thus late, and usually carries the message
of indelible Israelite identity only by implication.[11] Nowhere is it as
clear as the virtually opposite claim "that the overt apostate is like a
non-Jew in all respects" (*y. Eruv.* 6.2). Similarly, the affinity of apostates
with non-Jews (who are sometimes seen as less culpable, *t. B. Metz.* 2)
and their ultimate fate in Gehenna (*t. Sanh.* 13:4–5; *b. Rosh Hash.* 17a)
are clearly and emphatically asserted.[12] One might also wonder
whether calling someone an apostate Jew (as in *Israel mumar*) is any
more than a convenient way of referring to where the person is from,
and not necessarily a way of defining where, in terms of Jewish identity,
he or she now is. An analogy could be with *Hermas,* which we discussed
above, where Christian apostates fall under the general heading of
"believers" but only, it seems, as a convenient way of referring to them.
It implies nothing about their current or future status, for they are said
to be beyond repentance and destined for eternal death. Of course,
even if we could identify a consistent rabbinic view—and on the issue
of apostates this would not be easy—it would not necessarily represent
the view of Jews as a whole during the period we are interested in. One
reason for this is that in early rabbinic sources apostasy is not a major
theme. With a touch of exaggeration, Cohen puts it like this:

> In particular the rabbis of the Middle Ages devoted a great deal of
> attention to the status of the Jew who crossed the boundary and

10. Porton makes the point repeatedly (1994:40, 75, 80, 177, 196), but using the
same basic evidence: *t. Demai* 2:5; *b. Bek.* 30b; the ruling that Jews could buy ritual
objects from a defecting proselyte (*y. Avod. Zar.* 2:2); and the suggestion that returning
apostates took precedence over new converts (*y. Hor.* 3:5).

11. Schiffman's argument (1985:48–49), for example, rests on the interpretation in
the Babylonian Talmud. The Sifra passage emphatically argues that apostates are not
part of the covenant because they have abandoned or transgressed it.

12. S. Stern presents this evidence, though drawing a somewhat different conclusion (1994:108–9). He recognizes, however, that the Israelite identity of apostates is seldom referred to and often only implicit.

became a gentile, one of Us who became one of Them. Ancient rabbinic law paid little attention to apostates, but in the Middle Ages, in
both the Christian and Islamic spheres, apostasy was a serious problem and demanded attention. Was the apostate a Jew? This was the
only major question for which the ancient legacy was entirely inade-
quate. (1999:343–44)

We may turn briefly to the question of numbers. Our trawl through
the evidence has turned up rather more examples of apostasy than are
usually recognized. Yet one could still argue that, spread over three or
four hundred years or more, they were relatively rare. This, however,
may simply be because apostasy was not a happy topic to dwell on.
Some of the evidence suggests that defection may have been far more
common than we have tended to think: the allusions in Philo to Jewish
apostates in Alexandria; the Jewish defectors in Suetonius; the
Christian defectors in *Hermas*'s Rome; and Pliny's Bithynia. The allusions are in all cases fleeting, but they may be the more telling for that.
They suggest that apostasy/defection were not the rare or isolated phenomena that some have supposed. If we follow the ancient sources, we
could clearly not argue that as fast as converts came in one door defectors left by another. Their numbers are significant enough, however, for
us to grant them a more prominent role in the religious life of the
ancient world than they have heretofore been given. It is worth noting
that most of the defectors, when specified, are male. This may be the
result of biased reporting, or a reflection of the patriarchal structure of
the ancient world, where, in the public realm, the activities of men were
considered more important. It is interesting nevertheless.

Boundaries and Competing Claims

The evidence surveyed here invites a few further reflections. It is pertinent to the issue of the competing claims of religious and quasi-religious
groups in the ancient world. As noted at the beginning, there is a sense in
which any convert to Judaism or Christianity could be labeled a defector
(from the other camp or from the pagan world at large). Conversion and
defection are two sides of the same coin. The ancient evidence, however,

is generally not interested in both sides at once, but focuses on one or the other. We have paid attention to sources that concentrate on the aspect of leaving, partly because to include both would unduly broaden the scope of this study and partly because the evidence for conversion has been extensively discussed. Nevertheless, the reasons given for defection, in ancient and modern sources, are, as some have noted, often a mirror image of the reasons that explain the attraction and retention of converts, so that studying the one is an indirect way of studying the other.

In most cases defection, like conversion, involved a more or less deliberate crossing of boundaries even when the shift was gradual rather than precipitate. In some instances, the reaction may have been mild. One can imagine, for example, that some of the gradual drifters excoriated by Philo were tolerated by other Alexandrian Jews, at least until (and if) they effectively renounced their allegiance to Judaism. But by and large defection was a rancorous business and provoked extreme reactions, understandably so in the case of those who became traitors or who turned violently on their former community. But even the less dramatic instances were deeply troubling. Converts were viewed with pride, but they merely confirmed what a community took for granted—the superiority of their claims. Defectors were deeply disturbing, for they implicitly undercut everything that the community stood for. Indeed, we might surmise that defectors were more disturbing than converts were comforting. The very act of defection was bad enough, but when it involved attachment to a rival group, as in some cases it did, the blow was doubled—as when Jews became Christians or Dionysians, or when Christians reverted to their Jewish or pagan past.

The sheer range and variety of defectors uncovered in our survey are striking. The multiple reasons and different processes they describe remind us of the complexity of the phenomena we study. It is easy to start out thinking that the boundaries among different communities will be clear-cut and the transgression of them obvious. Yet they are never as distinct as we sometimes want to make them. Boundaries, in the normal conditions of social life, would have been more like penumbras than hard-and-fast lines. That we cannot always be sure that we are dealing with defectors (apostates) rather than deviants (heretics) is itself sufficient evidence of this. The epigraphic evidence for Jewish defectors is often ambiguous in this way, as are some of Philo's reports of disaffected Jews. The matter is complicated by the question of who draws the boundaries. In the ancient evidence, it is mostly those who oppose or condemn defectors, not the defectors themselves. Mostly, too, we learn only about overt acts and not internal motivations. Indeed, it is interesting to note that defection is defined in many cases more by actions than by beliefs, even in the supposedly more belief-oriented Christian tradition. Yet, partly no doubt because actions are an expression of convictions, neither Jewish nor Christian evidence allows a consistent distinction, say, between deviants who believe the wrong things and defectors who do them.

BIBLIOGRAPHY

Albrecht, S. L., Marie Cornwall, and Perry H. Cunningham. 1988. "Religious Leave-Taking: Disengagement and Disaffiliation among Mormons." In Bromley 1988:62–80.

Alexander, Loveday. 1994. "Paul and the Hellenistic Schools: The Evidence of Galen." In Engberg-Pedersen 1994:60–83.

Applebaum, S. 1976. "The Social and Economic Status of the Jews in the Diaspora." In *The Jewish People in the First Century,* vol. 2: *Historical Geography, Political History, Social, Cultural and Religious Life and Institutions,* edited by S. Safrai and M. Stern, 701–27. CRINT 1/2. Philadelphia: Fortress Press.

———. 1979. *Jews and Greeks in Ancient Cyrene.* SJLA 28. Leiden: Brill.

Ascough, Richard, S. 1998. *What Are They Saying about the Formation of the Pauline Churches?* New York: Paulist.

Assaraf, Albert. 1991. *L'Hérétique: Elicha ben Abuyah ou l'autre absolu.* Collection Métafora. Paris: Ballard.

Ayali, Meir. 1988–89. "Die Apostasie des Elischa ben Abuyah." *Kairos* 30-31:31–40.

Barclay, John M. G. 1995a. "Deviance and Apostasy: Some Applications of Deviance Theory to First-Century Judaism and Christianity." In *Modelling Early Christianity: Social Scientific Studies of the New Testament in Its Context,* edited by Philip F. Esler, 114–27. London: Routledge.

———. 1995b. "Paul among Diaspora Jews: Anomaly or Apostate?" *JSNT* 60:89–120.

———. 1996. *The Jews in the Mediterranean Diaspora: From Alexander to Trajan (323 BCE—117 CE).* Edinburgh: T. & T. Clark.

———. 1998. "Who Was Considered an Apostate in the Jewish Diaspora?" In Stanton and Stroumsa, 1998:80–98.

Bardy, Gustave. 1949. *La Conversion au Christianisme durant les premiers siècles.* Théologie 15. Paris: Aubier.

Barker, Eileen. 1985. "Defection from the Unification Church: Some Statistics and Distinctions." In Bromley 1985:166–84.

———.1998. "Standing at the Cross-Roads: The Politics of Marginality in 'Subversive' Organizations." In Bromley 1998b:75–93.

Barnes, Jonathan. 1989. "Antiochus of Ascalon." In *Philosophia Togata: Essays on Philosophy and Roman Society,* edited by Miriam Griffin and Jonathan Barnes, 51–96. Oxford: Clarendon.

Baron, Salo Wittmayer. 1952. *A Social and Religious History of the Jews.* 3 vols. New York: Columbia Univ. Press.

Bauckham, Richard. 1985. "The Two Fig Tree Parables in the Apocalypse of Peter." *JBL* 104:269–87.

———. 1988. "The Apocalypse of Peter: An Account of Research." In *ANRW* II.25.6:4712–50.

———. 1994. "The *Apocalypse of Peter:* A Jewish Christian Apocalypse from the Time of Bar Kokhba." *Apocrypha* 5:7–111.

———. 1998. "Jews and Jewish Christians in the Land of Israel at the Time of the Bar Kochba War, with Special Reference to the *Apocalypse of Peter.*" In Stanton and Strousma, 1998:228–37.

Begg, Christopher. 1997. "Solomon's Apostasy (1 Kings 11,13) according to Josephus." *JSJ* 28:294–313.

Bernand, André. 1972. *Le Paneion d'el Kanaïs: Les Inscriptiones grecques.* Leiden: Brill.

Betz, Hans Dieter. 1979. *Galatians.* Hermeneia. Philadelphia: Fortress Press.

Bévenot, Maurice, editor. 1971. *Cyprian: De Lapsis and De Ecclesiae Catholicae Unitate*. OECT. Oxford: Clarendon.

Bickerman, Elias. 1975. *The God of the Maccabees: Studies in the Meaning and Origin of the Maccabean Revolt*. Trans. Horst J. Moehring. SJLA 32. Leiden: Brill.

Borgen, Peder. 1995. "'Yes,' 'No,' 'How Far?' The Participation of Jews and Christians in Pagan Cults." In Engberg-Pedersen 1995:30–59.

Brinkerhoff, Merlin B., and M. L. Mackie. 1992. "Casting off the Bonds of Organized Religion: A Religious-Careers Approach to the Study of Apostasy." *RRelRes* 34:235–53.

Bromley, David G., editor. 1988. *Falling from the Faith: Causes and Consequences of Religious Apostasy*. Beverly Hills, Calif.: Sage.

———. 1998a. "The Social Construction of Contested Exit Roles: Defectors, Whistleblowers, and Apostates." In Bromley 1998b:19–47.

———, editor. 1998b. *The Politics of Religious Apostasy: The Role of Apostates in the Transformation of Religious Movements*. Westport, Conn.: Praeger.

Brown, Peter. 2000. *The Rise of Western Christendom: Triumph and Diversity, A.D. 200–1000*. The Making of Europe. Cambridge, Mass.: Blackwell.

Brox, N. 1984. "Häresie." In *RAC* 13:248–97.

Buchholz, Dennis D. 1988. *Your Eyes Will Be Opened: A Study of the Greek (Ethiopic) Apocalypse of Peter*. SBLDS 97. Atlanta: Scholars.

Burkert, Walter. 1982. "Craft Versus Sect: The Problem of Orphics and Pythagoreans." In *Jewish and Christian Self-Definition*, vol. 3: *Self-Definition in the Greco-Roman World*, edited by Ben F. Meyer and E. P. Sanders, 1–22. Philadelphia: Fortress Press.

Cancik, Hubert. 1997. "The History of Culture, Religion, and Institutions in Ancient Historiography: Philological Observations Concerning Luke's History." *JBL* 116:673–95.

Carter, Lewis F. 1998. "Carriers of Tales: On Assessing Credibility of Apostate and Other Outsider Accounts of Religious Practices." In Bromley 1998b:221–37.

Charlesworth, James H., editor. 1983–85. *The Old Testament Pseudepigrapha*. 2 vols. New York: Doubleday.

Bibliography **139**

Clay, Diskin. 1998. "The Cults of Epicurus," in *Paradosis and Survival: Three Chapters in the History of Epicurean Philosophy*, 75–102. Ann Arbor: Univ. of Michigan Press.

Cohen, Shaye J. D. 1980. "A Virgin Defiled: Some Rabbinic and Christian Views on the Origins of Heresy." *USQR* 36:1–11.

———. 1989. "Crossing the Boundary and Becoming a Jew." *HTR* 82:13–33.

———. 1990. "Religion, Ethnicity and 'Hellenism' in the Emergence of Jewish Identity in Maccabean Palestine." In *Religion and Religious Practice in the Seleucid Kingdom*, edited by Per Bilde et al., 204–23. Aarhus: Aarhus Univ. Press.

———. 1994. "*Ioudaios to genos* and Related Expressions in Josephus." In *Josephus and the History of the Greco-Roman Period: Essays in Memory of Morton Smith*, edited by Fausto Parente and Joseph Sievers, 23–38. StPB 41. Leiden: Brill.

———. 1999. *The Beginnings of Jewishness: Boundaries, Varieties, Uncertainties*. Hellenistic Culture and Society 31. Berkeley: Univ. of California Press.

Collins, John J. 1983. *Between Athens and Jerusalem: Jewish Identity in the Hellenistic Diaspora*. New York: Crossroad.

Colson, F. H., translator. 1985. *Philo.* Vol. 9. LCL. Cambridge, Mass.: Harvard Univ. Press.

Cook, John Granger. 2002. *The Interpretation of the New Testament in Greco-Roman Paganism*. Peabody, Mass: Hendrickson.

Croke, Brian, and Jill Harries, editors. 1982. *Religious Conflict in Fourth-Century Rome: A Documentary Study*. Sydney: Sydney Univ. Press.

Curbera, J. B. 1996. "Jewish Names from Sicily." *ZPE* 115:257–60.

deSilva, David A. 1996. "Exchanging Favor for Wrath: Apostasy in Hebrews and Patron-Client Relationships." *JBL* 115:91–116.

Desjardins, Michel R. 1991. "Bauer and Beyond: On Recent Scholarly Discussions of *hairesis* in the Early Christian Era." *SecCent* 8:65–82.

Devda, Tomasz. 1997. "Did the Jews Use the Name Moses in Antiquity?" *ZPE* 115:257–60.

Droge, Arthur J., and James D. Tabor. 1992. *A Noble Death: Suicide and Martydom among Christians and Jews in Antiquity*. San Francisco: Harper.

Dunn, James D. G. 1998. "Paul: Apostate or Apostle of Israel?" *ZNW* 89:256–71.

Edwards, Mark. 1993. "Ammonius, Teacher of Origen." *JEH* 44:169–81.

Edwards, Mark J. 1989. "Satire and Verisimilitude: Christianity in Lucian's *Peregrinus.*" *Historia* 38:89–98.

Endelman, Todd M. 1987. *Jewish Apostasy in the Modern World.* New York: Holmes and Meir.

Engberg-Pedersen, Troels, editor. 1995. *Paul in His Hellenistic Context.* Minneapolis: Fortress Press.

Etienne, Stéphane. 2000. "Réflexion sur l'apostasie de Tibérius Julius Alexander." *Studia Philonica Annual* 12:122–42.

Feldman, Louis H. 1960. "The Orthodoxy of the Jews in Hellenistic Egypt." *JSocSt* 22:215–37.

———. 1986. "How Much Hellenism in Jewish Palestine?" *HUCA* 57:83–111.

———. 1993. *Jew and Gentile in the Ancient World: Attitudes and Interactions from Alexander to Justinian.* Princeton: Princeton Univ. Press.

Figueras, Paul. 1990. "Epigraphic Evidence for Proselytism in Ancient Judaism." *Immanuel* 24/5:194–206.

Freudenberger, Rudolf. 1969. *Das Verhalten der römischen Behörden gegen die Christen im 2 Jahrhundert dargestellt am Brief des Plinius an Trajan und das Reskripten Trajans und Hadrians.* MBPF 52. Munich: Beck.

Frischer, Bernard. 1982. *The Sculpted Word: Epicureanism and Philosophical Recruitment in Ancient Greece.* Berkeley: Univ. of California Press.

Gaston, Lloyd. 1987. *Paul and the Torah.* Vancouver: Univ. of British Columbia Press.

Glad, Clarence E. 1995. *Paul and Philodemus: Adaptability in Epicurean and Early Christian Psychagogy.* NovTSup 81. Leiden: Brill.

Goodenough, Erwin R. 1956. "The Bosphorus Inscriptions to the Most High God." *JQR* 47:221–44.

Goodman, Martin. 1989. "Nerva, the *Fiscus Judaicus* and Jewish Identity." *JRS* 79:40–44.

———. 1994a. "Jews and Judaism in the Mediterranean Diaspora in the Late Roman Period: The Limitations of Evidence." *Journal of Mediterranean Studies* 4:208–24.

———. 1994b. "Josephus as Roman Citizen." In *Josephus and the History of the Greco-Roman Period: Essays in Memory of Morton Smith,* edited by Fausto Parente and Joseph Sievers, 329–38. StPB 41. Leiden: Brill.

———. 1996. "The Function of the Minim in Early Rabbinic Judaism." In *Geschichte—Tradition—Reflexion: Festschrift für Martin Hengel zum 70. Geburtstag,* 3 vols., edited by Peter P. Schäfer, 1.501–10. Tübingen: Mohr/Siebeck.

Goshen-Gottstein, Alon. 2000. *The Sinner and the Amnesiac: The Rabbinic Invention of Elisha Ben Abuyah and Eleazer Ben Arach.* Contraversions. Stanford: Stanford Univ. Press.

Grabbe, Lester L. 1992. *Judaism from Cyrus to Hadrian.* 2 vols. Minneapolis: Fortress Press.

Green, Henry A. 1985. *The Economic and Social Origins of Gnosticism: Assimilation and Apostasy.* SBLDS 77. Atlanta: Scholars.

Gruen, Erich S. 2002. *Diaspora: Jews Amidst Greeks and Romans.* Cambridge: Harvard Univ. Press.

Guignebert, Charles. 1923. "Les Demi-Chrétiens et l'Eglise Antique." *RHR* 88:65–102.

Hadas-Lebel, Mireille. 1973. *De Providentia 1 & 2: Les oeuvres de Philon d'Alexandrie.* Paris: Cerf.

Hadaway, C. Kirk. 1989. "Identifying American Apostates: A Cluster Analysis." *JSSR* 28:210–15.

Hall, John R., and Philip Schuyler. 1998. "Apostasy, Apocalypse, and Religious Violence: An Exploratory Comparison of Peoples Temple, the Branch Davidians, and the Solar Temple." In Bromley 1998b:141–69.

Harland, Philip. 2003. *Associations, Synagogues, and Congregations. Claiming A Place in Ancient Mediterranean Society.* Minneapolis: Fortress Press.

Harmon, A. M. 1936. *Lucian*. LCL. Vol. 5. New York: Putnam.

Harvey, A. E. 1985. "Forty Strokes Save One: Social Aspects of Judaizing and Apostasy." In *Alternative Approaches to New Testament Study*, edited by A. E. Harvey, 79–96. London: SPCK.

Hayes, Christine. 1999. "Intermarriage and Impurity in Ancient Jewish Sources." *HTR* 92:3–36.

Hengel, Martin. 1974. *Judaism and Hellenism: Studies in Their Encounter in Palestine during the Early Hellenistic Period.* 2 vols. Translated by John Bowden. Philadelphia: Fortress Press.

Henten, Jan Willem van, and Alice J. Bij de Vaate. 1996. "Jewish or Non-Jewish? Some Remarks on the Identification of Jewish Inscriptions in Asia Minor." *BO* 53:16–28.

Hicks, R. D. 1925. *Diogenes Laertius: Lives of Eminent Philosophers*. LCL. New York: Putnam.

Hillgarth, J. N., editor. 1986. *Christianity and Paganism, 350–750: The Conversion of Western Europe.* The Middle Ages. Philadelphia: Univ. of Pennsylvania Press.

Hoge, Dean R. 1988. "Why Catholics Drop Out." In Bromley 1988:81–99.

Holmes, Michael W. 1992. *The Apostolic Fathers: Greek Texts and English Translations of Their Writings.* J. B. Lightfoot and J. R. Harmer, translators and editors. Edited and revised by Michael Holmes. Grand Rapids: Baker.

Horbury, William. 1982. "The Benediction of the *minim* and Early Jewish-Christian Controversy." *JTS* 33:19–61.

Horbury, William, and David Noy, editors. 1992. *Jewish Inscriptions of Graeco-Roman Egypt.* Cambridge: Cambridge Univ. Press.

Horsley, G. H. R. 1981. *New Documents Illustrating Early Christianity: A Review of the Greek Inscriptions and Papyri Published in 1976.* Vol. 1. North Ryde, N.S.W.: Macquarie Univ.

———. 1987. *New Documents Illustrating Early Christianity: A Review of the Greek Inscriptions and Papyri Published in 1979.* Vol. 4. North Ryde, N.S.W.: Macquarie Univ.

Horst, P. W. van der. 1991. *Ancient Jewish Epitaphs.* Kampen: Kok.

Hunsberger, Bruce. 1980. "A Reexamination of the Antecedents of Apostasy." *RRelRes* 21:158–70.

————. 1983. "Apostasy: A Social Learning Perspective." *RRelRes* 25:21–38.

Jacobs, Janet Liebman. 1989. *Divine Disenchantment: Deconverting from New Religions.* Bloomington: Indiana Univ. Press.

Janowitz, Naomi. 1998. "Rabbis and their Opponents: The Construction of the 'Min' in Rabbinic Anecdotes." *JECS* 6:449–62.

Jeffers, James S. 1991. *Conflict at Rome: Social Order and Hierarchy in Early Christianity.* Minneapolis: Fortress Press.

Johnson, Daniel Carson. 1998. "Apostates Who Never Were: The Social Construction of *Absque Facto* Apostate Narratives." In Bromley 1998b:115–37.

Jones, Brian W. 1992. *The Emperor Domitian.* London: Routledge.

Kalmin, Richard. 1994. "Christians and Heretics in Rabbinic Literature of Late Antiquity." *HTR* 87:155–69.

Kant, Laurence H. 1987. "Jewish Inscriptions in Greek and Latin." In *ANRW* II.20.2:671–713.

Karabelias, E. 1994. "Apostasie et dissidence religeuse à Byzance de Justinien Ier jusqu'à l'invasion arabe (variations byzantines sur l'intolerance)." *Islamochristiana* 20:41–74.

Kerkeslager, Allen. 1997. "Maintaining Jewish Identity in the Greek Gymnasium: A 'Jewish Load' in CPJ 3.159 (= P.Schub. 37 = P.Berol. 13406)." *JSJ* 28:12–23.

Kinzig, Wolfram. 1998. "War der Neuplatoniker Porphyrios ursprünglich Christ?" In *Mousopolos Stephanos: Festschrift für Herwig Görgermanns,* edited by M. Baumbach et al., 320–32. Heidelberg: Winter.

Klassen, William. 1996. *Judas: Betrayer or Friend of Jesus?* Minneapolis: Fortress Press.

Kraabel, A. Thomas. 1982 "The Roman Diaspora: Six Questionable Assumptions." *JJS* 33:445–64.

Kraemer, Ross S. 1989. "On the Meaning of the Term 'Jew' in Greco-Roman Inscriptions." *HTR* 82:35-53

————. 1991. "Jewish Tuna and Christian Fish: Identifying Religious Affiliation in Epigraphic Sources." *HTR* 84:141–62.

Lake, Kirsopp. 1926. *Eusebius. The Ecclesiastical History*. Cambridge: Harvard Univ. Press.

Lampe, Peter. 2003. *From Paul to Valentinus: Christians at Rome in the First Two Centuries*. Trans. Michael Steinhauser. Minneapolis: Fortress Press.

Le Bohec, Yann. 1981. "Inscriptions Juives et Judaïsantes de L'Afrique Romaine." *Antiquités africaines* 17:165–207.

Le Boulluec, Alain. 1985. *La notion d'hérésie dans la littérature grecque (IIe—IIIe siècles)*. 2 vols. Paris: Études Augustiniennes.

Levinskaya, Irina. 1996. *The Book of Acts in Its Diaspora Setting*. The Book of Acts in Its First Century Setting 5. Grand Rapids: Eerdmans.

Lewis, D. M. 1957. "The First Greek Jew." *JSS* 2:264–66.

Lifshitz, Baruch. 1962. "Beitrage zur palästinschen Epigraphik." *ZDPV* 78:64–88.

Linder, Amnon. 1987. *The Jews in Roman Imperial Legislation*. Detroit: Wayne State Univ. Press.

Lübbe, J. 1986. "A Reinterpretation of 4Q Testimonia." *RevQ* 12:187–97.

Maccoby, Hyam. 1992. *Judas Iscariot and the Myth of Jewish Evil*. London: Peter Habban.

MacDonald, Margaret Y. 2003. "Was Celsus Right? The Role of Women in the Exapansion of Early Christianity." In *Early Christian Families in Context: A Cross-Disciplinary Dialogue*, edited by David Balch and Carolyn Osiek, 140–67. Grand Rapids: Eerdmans.

MacMullen, Ramsay. 1984. *Christianizing the Roman Empire, A.D. 100–400*. New Haven: Yale Univ. Press.

———. 1997. *Christianity and Paganism in the Fourth to the Eighth Centuries*. New Haven: Yale Univ. Press.

Maier, Harry O. 1991. *The Social Setting of the Ministry as Reflected in the Writings of Hermas, Clement, and Ignatius*. Dissertations, Studies in Religion 1. Waterloo: Wilfrid Laurier Univ. Press.

Marshall, I. Howard 1987. "The Problem of Apostasy in the New Testament." *Perspectives in Religious Studies* 14:65–80.

Martin, Troy W. 1995. "Apostasy to Paganism: The Rhetorical Stasis of the Galatian Controversy." *JBL* 114:437–61.

Mason, Steve N. 1996. " PHILOSOPHIAI: Graeco-Roman, Judean and Christian." In *Voluntary Associations in the Graeco-Roman World*, eds. John S. Kloppenborg and Stephen G. Wilson, 31–58. London: Routledge.

Mauss, Armand L. 1969. "Dimensions of Religious Defection." *RRelRes* 10:128–35.

Mendelson, Alan. 1988. *Philo's Jewish Identity.* BJS 161. Atlanta: Scholars.

Millar, Fergus. 1983. "Epigraphy." In *Sources for Ancient History*, edited by Michael Crawford, 80–136. Cambridge: Cambridge Univ. Press.

Mitchell, Stephen. 1993. *Anatolia: Land, Men and Gods in Asia Minor.* Vol. 2. Oxford: Clarendon.

Modrzejewski, Joseph Mélèze. 1993. "How to Be a Greek and Yet a Jew in Hellenistic Alexandria." In *Diasporas in Antiquity*, edited by Shaye J. D. Cohen and Ernest S. Frerichs, 65–91. BJS 288. Atlanta: Scholars.

Moles, J. L. 1978. "The Career and Conversion of Dio Chrysostom." *JHS* 98:79–100.

Musurillo, Herbert. 1972. *The Acts of the Christian Martyrs.* OECT. Oxford: Clarendon.

Nock, Arthur Darby. 1933. *Conversion: The Old and the New in Religion from Alexander the Great to Augustine of Hippo.* Oxford: Clarendon.

Noy, David. 1993–95. *Jewish Inscriptions of Western Europe.* 2 vols. Cambridge: Cambridge Univ. Press.

Oropeza, B. J. 2000. *Paul and Apostasy: Eschatology, Perseverance, and Falling Away in the Corinthian Congregation.* WUNT 2/115. Tübingen: Mohr/Siebeck.

Porton, Gary G. 1994. *The Stranger within Your Gates: Converts and Conversion in Rabbinic Literature.* CSHJ. Chicago: Univ. of Chicago Press.

Rajak, Tessa, and David Noy. 1993. "*Archisynagogoi*: Office, Title and Social Status in the Graeco-Jewish Synagogue." *JRS* 83: 80–98.

Ramsay, W. M. 1897. *Cities and Bishoprics of Phrygia*. Vol 1, Part 2. Oxford: Clarendon.

Rowland, Christopher. 1982. *The Open Heaven: A Study of Apocalyptic in Judaism and Early Christianity*. New York: Crossroad.

Rutgers, L. V. 1995. *The Jews in Late Ancient Rome: Evidence of Cultural Interaction in the Roman Diaspora*. RGRW 126. Leiden: Brill.

———. 1997. "Interaction and Its Limits: Some Notes on the Jews of Sicily in Late Antiquity." *ZPE* 115:245–56.

Sandelin, Karl-Gustav. 1991. "The Danger of Idolatry according to Philo." *Temenos* 27:109–50.

Sanders, E. P. 1977. *Paul and Palestinian Judaism: A Comparison of Patterns of Religion*. Philadelphia: Fortress Press.

Sanders, Jack T. 1993. *Schismatics, Sectarians, Dissidents, Deviants: The First One Hundred Years of Jewish-Christian Relations*. Valley Forge, Pa.: Trinity.

Schäfer, Peter. 1981. *Der Bar-Kokhba Aufstand: Studien zum zweiten jüdischen Krieg gegen Rom*. TSAJ 1. Tübingen: Mohr/Siebeck.

Schiffman, Lawrence H. 1985. *Who Was a Jew? Rabbinic and Halakhic Perspectives on the Jewish-Christian Schism*. Hoboken, N.J.: Ktav.

Schlier, Heinrich. 1964. "Hairesis." In *TDNT* 1:180–84.

Schroeder, F. M. 1987. "Ammonius Saccas." In *ANRW* II.36.495–506.

Schürer, Emil. 1973–87. *The History of the Jewish People in the Age of Jesus Christ (175 B.C.—A.D. 135)*. 3 vols. in 4. Edited and revised by Geza Vermes, Fergus Millar, Matthew Black, and Martin Goodman. Edinburgh: T. & T. Clark.

Sedley, David. 1976. "Epicurus and His Professional Rivals." In *Etudes sur l'Epicurisme antique*, edited by Jean Bollack and André Laks, 121–60. Cahiers de Philologie 1. Lille: Publications de l'Université de Lille III.

———. 1989. "Philosophical Allegiance in the Greco-Roman World." In *Philosophia Togata: Essays on Philosophy and Roman Society*, edited by Miriam Griffin and Jonathan Barnes, 97–119. Oxford: Clarendon.

Segal, Alan F. 1977. *Two Powers in Heaven: Early Rabbinic Reports about Christianity and Gnosticism*. SJLA 25. Leiden: Brill.

————. 1990. *Paul the Convert: The Apostolate and Apostasy of Saul the Pharisee.* New Haven: Yale Univ. Press.

Seland, Torrey. 1995. *Establishment Violence in Philo and Luke: A Study of Non-Conformity to the Torah and Jewish Vigilante Reactions.* BibIntSer 15. Leiden: Brill.

Shepherd, A. R. R. 1979. "Jews, Christian and Heretics in Acmonia and Eumeneia." *Anatolian Studies* 24:169–80.

Sherkat, Darren E., and John Wilson. 1995. "Preferences, Constraints, and Choices in Religious Markets: An Examination of Religious Switching and Apostasy." *Social Forces* 73:993–1026.

Shupe, Anson. 1998. "The Role of Apostates in the North American Anticult Movement." In Bromley 1998b:209–17.

Simon, Marcel. 1979. "From Greek Hairesis to Christian Heresy." In *Early Christian Literature and the Classical Intellectual Tradition: In honorem Robert M. Grant,* edited by William R. Schoedel and Robert L. Wilken, 101–16. Théologie historique 53. Paris: Beauchesne.

Smallwood, E. Mary. 1976. *The Jews under Roman Rule from Pompey to Diocletian.* SJLA 20. Leiden: Brill.

Smith, Jonathan Z. 1982. "Fences and Neighbors: Some Contours of Early Judaism." In *Imagining Religion: From Babylon to Jonestown,* 1–18. CSHJ. Chicago: Univ. of Chicago Press.

Smith, Rowland B. E. 1995. *Julian's Gods: Religion and Philosophy in the Thought and Action of Julian the Apostate.* London: Routledge.

Solin, Heikki. 1983. "Juden und Syrer im westlichen Teil der römischen Welt: Eine ethnisch-demographische Studie mit besonderer Berhchsichtigung der sprächlichen Zustände." In *ANRW* II.29.2:587–789.

Staden, Heinrich von. 1982. "Hairesis and Heresy: The Case of the *haireseis iatrikai.*" In *Jewish and Christian Self-Definition,* vol. 3: *Self-Definition in the Greco-Roman World,* edited by Ben F. Meyer and E. P. Sanders, 76–100. Philadelphia: Fortress Press.

Stanton, Graham N., and Guy G. Stroumsa, editors. 1998. *Tolerance and Intolerance in Early Judaism and Christianity.* Cambridge: Cambridge Univ. Press.

Stark, Rodney. 1996. *The Rise of Christianity: A Sociologist Reconsiders History.* Princeton: Princeton Univ. Press.

Stern, Menahem. 1984. *Greek and Latin Authors on Jews and Judaism.* Jerusalem: Israel Academy of Sciences and Humanities.

Stern, Sacha. 1994. *Jewish Identity in Early Rabbinic Writings.* AGJU 23. Leiden: Brill.

Stroumsa, Guy G. 1981. "Aḥer: A Gnostic." In *The Rediscovery of Gnosticism,* vol. 2: *Sethian Gnosticism,* edited by Bentley Layton, 808–18. Studies in the History of Religions 41. Leiden: Brill.

Tcherikover, Victor A. 1957. *Corpus Papyrorum Judicarum.* Vol. 1. Cambridge: Harvard Univ. Press.

Thoma, Clemens. 1990. "Die Christen in rabbinischer Optik: Heiden, Häretiker oder Fromme?" In *Christlicher Antijüdaismus und jüdischer Antipaganismus,* edited by Herbert Frohnhofen, 23–49. Hamburg: Steinmann & Steinmann.

Thompson, Leonard L. 1990. *The Book of Revelation: Apocalypse and Empire.* Oxford: Oxford Univ. Press.

Tomson, Peter J. 1986. "The Names Israel and Jew in Ancient Judaism and in the New Testament." *Bijdragen, Tijdschrift voor Filosofie en Theologie* 47:120–40, 266–89.

Trebilco, Paul R. 1991. *Jewish Communities in Asia Minor.* SNTSMS 69. Cambridge: Cambridge Univ. Press.

Turner, E. G. 1954. "Tiberius Iulius Alexander." *JRS* 44:54–64.

Unnik, W. C. van. 1974. "Josephus' Account of the Story of Israel's Sin with Alien Women in the Country of Midian (Num. 25:1ff.)." In *Travels in the World of the Old Testament: Festschrift for M. A. Beek,* edited by M. S. H. G. Heerma van Voss et al., 241–61. Assen: Van Gorcum.

Walzer, Richard. 1949. *Galen on Jews and Christians.* OCPM. London: Oxford Univ. Press.

Whittaker, Molly. 1984. *Jews and Christians: Graeco-Roman Views.* Cambridge: Cambridge Univ. Press.

Wilken, Robert L. 1971. "Collegia, Philosophical Schools and Theology." In *The Catacombs and the Colosseum: The Roman Empire as the Setting of Primitive Christianity,* ed Stephen Benko and John J. O'Rourke, 268–91. Valley Forge, Pa.: Judson.

————.1984. *The Christians as the Romans Saw Them*. New Haven: Yale Univ. Press.

Williams, M. H. 1990. "Domitian, The Jews and 'Judaizers'—A Simple Matter of *Cupiditas* and *Maiestas*?" *Historia* 39:196–211.

————. 1997a. "Jewish Use of Moses as a Personal Name in Graeco-Roman Antiquity—A Note." *ZPE* 118:274.

————. 1997b. "The Meaning and Function of *Ioudaios* in Graeco-Roman Inscriptions." *ZPE* 116:249–62.

Wilson, Stephen G. 1992. "Gentile Judaizers." *NTS* 38:605–16.

————. 1995. *Related Strangers: Jews and Christians 70–170 CE*. Minneapolis: Fortress Press.

Wise, Michael Owen. 1990. *A Critical Study of the Temple Scroll from Qumran Cave 11*. SAOC 49. Chicago: Oriental Institute of the Univ. of Chicago.

Wolfson, Harry A. 1947. *Philo: Foundations of Religious Philosophy in Judaism, Christianity, and Islam*. 2 vols. Cambridge: Harvard Univ. Press.

Wright, Stuart A. 1987. *Leaving Cults: The Dynamics of Defection*. Washington, D.C.: Society for the Scientific Study of Religion.

Wright, W. C. 1923. *The Works of the Emperor Julian*. LCL. Cambridge: Harvard.

Yadin, Yigael. 1977–83. *The Temple Scroll*. 3 vols. in 4. Jerusalem: Israel Exploration Society.

Zeitlin, Solomon. 1963–64. "Mumar and Meshumad." *JQR* 54:84–86.

INDEX OF ANCIENT SOURCES

INDEX OF MODERN AUTHORS